Transforming Tragedy:

Finding Growth Following Life's Traumas

Edward J. Hickling, Psy.D.

ISBN: 1477506896
ISBN 13: 9781477506899
CreateSpace, North Charleston, SC

Dedication

To Linda

Here at the frontier, there are falling leaves,
Although my neighbors are all barbarians,
And you, you are a thousand miles away...
There are always two cups at my table.

- Anonymous, T'ang Dynasty 618 - 906 A.D.

Contents

Acknowledgements

This book has been the culmination of several years of work. From a germ of an idea that came when I started to see that more than pain could follow a trauma, to seeing the strength that is present in nearly all of us, a great deal has gone into this book.

This work is best thought of as a living, growing document. As I have changed and grown, for both professional and personal reasons (as will be made clear in the book), my views, my understanding, and my way of seeing nearly everything has also changed. I constantly want to go back and redo certain parts of the book each time I read it or give lectures on the material. But like any document, the time comes to say "enough", and that is where it is at this time.

I have to acknowledge the considerable help that has been so graciously given to me in the completion of the book.

First, to all the people I have seen in my office: my patients (and my friends) who have had to deal with life's tragedies and traumas. They have been the best teachers of all. Their lives have shown me so much more than any book or journal that I've read, all of which pales next to what they shared in the privacy of my office. The honesty, vulnerability, and humanness exposed in that setting and the chance to learn as a healer and psychologist in the therapy setting, is an incredibly precious gift. I only hope that in my efforts to render care and help, that I have been worthy of that trust. I know I have endeavored to share and help in an equally honest fashion.

I have witnessed changes in myself over time. I know that the time I've shared with my patients along the way has been impacted by those patients who have gone before them in my journey as a practicing psychologist. These experiences have continued to impact my thinking in how I try to understand what it is to be human and how to help those who seek my help.

Several invaluable resources have furthered the work in this book. I am extremely fortunate to share in the intellect and brilliance of many people. To P., whose willingness to honestly share herself in her words, and in the words of great authors, I thank you. You have truly opened up doors that I never knew existed. While I have read many of the great works shared in this book, yours was the voice that led me to understand many of those words, and to be open to the depth of understanding in those authors and philosophers including those I had never heard of.

To my colleagues, Drs. Edward and Cris Blanchard, Loretta Malta, and Carol O'Brien; your comments and willingness to share ideas have greatly shaped the content and format of this book. It and I are unquestionably better for your insights and experiences. Whenever I had doubts about my grasp of an idea or concept, or how to share ideas or complicated concepts, you were there to make sure it was done as well as possible. Thank you.

To my family, Michael and Linda, for the reading and re-reading of words (Matt, I know you were there too, but I am glad you were deep in your own studies); Thank you for making sure the words made sense, and I didn't lose my direction too often. And thank you for the time it took to craft all of the work into this book. That time was time you also gave up from our time together. That is a gift of love and understanding that only comes when one knows the passions that each of us share.

And finally, to the doctors, professionals and people who have touched me in my life at times of great need. To Roberta Flesh, MD, my internist who is also a great humanitarian. I loved watching you meet with people including myself in your office. The degree of compassion, respect and humanity toward each of us in our moments of need was an inspiration I don't think I ever got to say to you. To Lisa Thorn, MD, who has demonstrated the same human qualities in a demanding profession. To Arthur Falk, MD, the surgeon I credit with saving my life following one of my own moments of trauma. Your skill was appreciated, but more so was your willingness to be there and to help someone you had just met in their most vulnerable time; you gave me a contrast to the other surgeons who instead typified much of what I see wrong with modern medicine. It was a true comfort when you came into a room, and your confidence and willingness to extend yourself to do everything possible to make sure of a positive outcome was a gift I always appreciated.

I have been very lucky. I have tried to be true with what has been shared. I hope that my experiences can be amplified with the input of so many, to give you the reader, something that will also help you move toward the life that you are hoping for.

EJH
9/1/12

Opening Remarks

"That which does not kill me, will only make me stronger"

- Friedrich Nietzsche, *Twilight of the Idols*

On January 14th 2007, I fell off my roof while trying to repair a leak. It happened in an instant. One moment I was checking my footing on the icy surface, intent on trying to get to a vent to see why water was coming in, the next, I was sliding off the roof. I remember trying to grab the gutter. I'm pretty sure I at least touched it, but I was falling too fast. I missed.

The next thing I recall was lying face down on the ground. I knew it was bad. I was messed up. My right arm did not work. Blood was coming out of my mouth. I could feel my feet, thought I could wiggle my toes, and I knew I was alive and thinking. But I was very aware this wasn't good. Surprisingly I didn't feel any pain. I remember thinking that was weird. And I knew vividly that there was a very good chance this was how I was going to die.

Fortunately, I was wrong, and I'm here to write this book.

Why write this Book?

A little over a year later, a lawyer I was doing some work for asked me a question. Knowing about the accident and that I'd done a lot of work with trauma victims, he asked, "Did all that you have learned as a psychologist help you deal with your own trauma?" I thought about that question several seconds before I answered. My answer was very certain. I said, "Yes. Everything I've learned over 25 years of working with trauma helped. I used it all and I learned even more as I faced my recovery every day".

I continued to think about that question a lot, and actually shifted some of my practice and research to answer a somewhat different but related question, "What exactly is it that I know which I can offer people not to just survive their personal life traumas, but perhaps to even thrive from such adverse times?" That's the question I try to answer in this book.

How are we going to do that? To begin, I have had the privilege and opportunity to treat the effects of the psychological impact of trauma for over 25 years. I have had the privilege of working with survivors of wars and POW camps when working at the Veterans Affairs Medical Center in Albany, NY. I have worked with people who have contracted horrible illnesses, some terminal, and tried to help as they and their families dealt with those events. I have worked with the survivors of rapes, assaults, plane crashes, train wrecks, 9/11 survivors, family members from the Lockerbie plane attack, natural disasters, horrible car crashes and just about any other kind of trauma one could confront. I have also been extremely fortunate to be part of some of the cutting edge psychological research centers, including the Center for Stress and Anxiety Disorders at SUNY Albany, where I was a Co-Principal Investigator with Dr. Edward B. Blanchard on several National Institute of Health (NIH) funded studies where we were able to assess and then develop treatments for posttraumatic stress disorder (PTSD) and other psychological problems that can frequently follow traumas.

Along the way I have been very lucky to learn from some of the world's best clinicians and thinkers in the field of medicine and psychology dealing with these problems on a regular basis. These relationships have taken me all over the world giving talks, and consulting and sharing our experiences internationally. I have also been able to share these insights with students, interns and fellows, who have constantly challenged and questioned conclusions and pushed for more and more knowledge that could help them and the people they work with.

One of the series of talks I gave grew into the related topic of how people often survive traumas successfully. This has included learning how some people, following their traumas, describe how out of their tragic events, that they were somehow able to find positive things that allowed them to grow from their horrors.

Last, I have always maintained a clinical practice, even when deeply involved in research and teaching. My best teachers without question have always been my patients, who have shared many hours and incredibly private events that have helped shape my understanding and appreciation of the humanness and wonder that's part of our makeup.

We are all much the same in these human qualities. The only edge a psychologist has is the opportunity to read and study about human behavior, seeing 30-40 people/week over decades and learning from them, and sharing in that human experience. We are all cut from the same cloth; all have a birth and a death; all seek the chance to try to live as well as we can. Values guide us, experience shapes us. Staying alive and open, even to pain, is difficult, yet it is something each of us must do if we are to live full and meaningful lives.

Nietzsche's quote which began this section has been used a great deal. It may even be true for some people. Similar ideas such as, "God wouldn't give me more than I could handle" have often been said at times of great despair. History and our literature have many examples of how, out of suffering, great wisdom and strength seem to appear.

Yet, we also have the very real experience where people have been broken by life. Where adversity has occurred, people are damaged, and they will never seem to be the same. A mother is lost following the death of a child, or a widow never gets past the loneliness that follows the death of her husband. We can be haunted by images, memories and emotions of tragic moments in life that forever color our experiences. What can we learn from those experiences, and how can we take from those tragedies insight that might provide help?

That has been the crux of my work, both in my clinical work and in my research efforts along the way.

This book is an effort at looking at what we know about the experiences that can follow trauma, what we know about the development and treatment of posttraumatic stress disorders, and about helping people get unstuck from those experiences that are intruding into the fabric of their everyday lives: their thoughts, feelings, and actions; what we have learned about the group of people who are seemingly resilient to life's tragedies; what we are learning about the potential for growth following traumas and tragic events. When we examine the differences and common threads among people, it is my experience and belief that there is a great deal that can be found to help all of us deal somewhat better with life's tragedies and traumas.

Along the way, I will share my own experience, and the experience of the thousands of patients who have shared so much of their lives with me in my work. Their identities will be protected even although as part of the research, waivers were signed allowing their stories to be told, unedited. My belief in protecting my patients' privacy holds me to that decision, even though some patients expressed a great willingness to have their identities revealed if it helped others. The examples and stories will continue to have the critical elements of those stories altered just enough to protect identities, while staying true to the information and lessons they shared so painfully.

The person lying there on the ground on January 14th 2007 was me. I will try to share that experience, and the experiences that followed, as best I can, where it makes sense. I will also try to blend that experience with decades of work and understanding of our current psychological knowledge and theories.

So this book presents several perspectives. The first is what we have learned to help people deal with psychological distress following trauma, particularly PTSD. The second is how people, who seem resilient to trauma, are able to achieve that and the lessons there that can help all of us do better. Third, is how we see that some people are able to actually grow from their trauma, and what we can learn from their knowledge and those stories. We will try to find the common threads in all three groups, in the similar but very different literature, and how that knowledge bears out from life's examples, my own, and the thousands of people I've had the chance to learn from, my patients.

The guiding purpose then is to share what we know from psychological literature, and what those who have suffered before us have to teach us. Or as the lawyer asked me, if all I had learned as a psychologist helped me to deal with my own trauma? Again the answer is a resounding, "Yes, it did".

I hope the book can offer you something to help you in your own personal traumas, and along the way share some of the very powerful experience of being human. We are amazing in our gifts and our strengths, much of which are revealed at those moments when life is especially hard and tragic. The rather large hope, is that this book can make each of us better able to transform those awful, terrifying moments into a more fulfilling, rich path for us all. Because, as much as we may wish it, life gives very few of us an existence free from pain and suffering.

A young man caught a small bird and held it behind his back. He then asked, "Master, is the bird I hold in my hands alive or dead? The boy thought this was a grand opportunity to play a trick on the old man. If the master answered "dead", it would be let loose into the air. If the master answered "alive" he would simply wring its neck. The master spoke, "The answer is in your hands"

- Anonymous

The Phoenix –

The Phoenix has been described as one of the most enduring images of transformation. The phoenix rises from the ashes anew. The phoenix is seen as a possible metaphor for all of us. From the ashes of our own personal tragedies and traumas, we can arise, anew, changed, transformed. We do not forget the events that have occurred to us, and we even carry scars of their occurrence. But as humans we have the amazing ability at times to take what ever it is that has been given for us to carry, and move forward towards a meaningful life. For some, that transformation allows us to become more of the kind of human being we would like to be. Our lessons often come with great costs. But having paid that price, some are able to move toward something that can arise from those fires, a transformed life. So, for this reason, we have used the phoenix as a symbol that is presented throughout the book, as a reminder of what is potentially inside all of us.

Chapter One

Trauma and Our Reactions
An Overview of Where We're Going

A **trauma** *is defined by Webster's Dictionary as, a bodily or mental injury usually caused by an external agent. A severe wound caused by a sudden physical or emotional shock causing lasting and substantial damage to a person's psychological development.*

A **tragedy** *is defined by Webster's Dictionary as, 1) a serious drama describing a conflict between the protagonist and a superior force (as destiny) and having a sad end that excites pity or terror, 2) a disastrous event, or 3) tragic quality or element.*

In this book we will use the terms somewhat interchangeably, but always aware of the distinct difference they can entail. A tragedy often is traumatic. A tragedy often includes a trauma; even though both tragedies and traumas can in certain situations stand-alone.

Life may give us tragedies. Tragedies and life's traumas may include catastrophic events, wars, motor vehicle accidents, sexual and physical assaults, natural disasters and death, among others.

What is important here is that while people, including psychologists, may argue over what event is "serious enough" to be labeled a trauma, each of us we knows when we have suffered a physical or mental injury. Whether the breakup of a relationship or hearing of the death of a loved one is a sufficient trauma to be judged as "equal to" those seen in war, or following rape or a major accident, is not a debate we need to enter. Our beginning place is one where we have suffered a painful event, one that we consider traumatic.

One could ask, how could a nice colonial house be the source of a trauma?

Well, I would answer, as I shared in the opening remarks, a house much like this one was the place of one of my traumas. What followed from my fall from the roof was

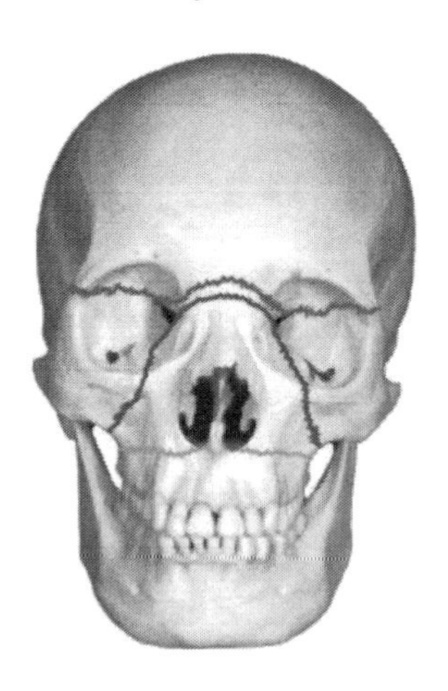

what is called a Lefort III fracture. Few people survive the fall I had. Even less survive without brain injury, or lasting neurological problems. I spent six weeks in the hospital. While I had tremendous doctors involved (I know, as I was on faculty at the medical center), two major surgeries, at least three near misses with death, and other moments to be shared later in this book, it was a time when I was certain of my death.

The second moment I'd like to share (the first was right after my fall) came on the way to the hospital. The ambulance crew was professional and did all they could along the way. Unfortunately, the ambulance crew had a new driver. He must have been distracted, because while he was clearly trying to get to the emergency department as fast as possible, he completely missed the entrance and drove right past it. I remember thinking, "Great, I'm going to die, because of this "F^#%*ng new guy" who doesn't even know how to get me to the door!"

What Do You Think?

One very important question we each need to ask ourselves is what do we think is a "normal reaction" to a very abnormal situation, a trauma or tragic event?

How you answer that determines how you see yourself (Am I normal? Am I broken? Am I weak?), and how you expect things to go (Will I ever get over this? Will I be the same, or different?).

There are **three** types of reactions people can have to trauma:

1) **Adverse Reactions:** They can become anxious, depressed, have images or memories of the trauma that won't leave them;

2) **Resilient Reactions:** They don't seem to have any reaction. They seem to be unaffected, tough, and just

keep on living the way they did before any trauma or tragedy had occurred;
3) **Growth Reactions:** They show some type of positive change. They seem to value life more, see the world and their place in it differently, and in some ways the trauma has actually added to the kind of person they are.

I have no doubt that I suffered a trauma on January 14, 2007 when I fell and was so severely injured. I was broken. I was afraid I would not get better. I was scared at times I would die. I knew at times I might die. Further, the trauma was not just the fall, and the broken bones, or even the fear. The trauma continued with new fears each day: the time I was told that there was a chance I wouldn't survive one of the operations; the days in rehabilitation when I had doubts I could ever return to care for my family; the worry that I would never be well enough to do even a simple push-up.

I have seen patients whose "traumas" included being told they had cancer and that they had little chance of surviving more than a year; soldiers who described the loss of their best friend, shot next to them when they were talking; and a woman raped by a "family friend" who kept coming over to visit. These events and how we react and deal with life's other traumas are what we will explore next.

The next few chapters will look at each of these reactions and try to show what we can take from them to help in the transformation of these life traumas.

SURPRISED BY JOY

Surprised by joy -impatient as the wind
I turned to share the transport - Oh! with whom
But Thee, deep buried in the silent tomb,
That spot which no vicissitude can find?
Love, faithful love, recalled thee to my mind –
But how could I forget thee? Through what power,
Even for the least division of an hour,
Have I been so beguiled as to be blind
To my most grievous loss? - That thought's return
Was the worst pang that sorrow ever bore
Save one, one only, when I stood forlorn,
Knowing my heart's best treasure was no more;
That neither present time, nor years unborn,
Could to my sight that heavenly face restore.

- William Wordsworth

Chapter Two

Adverse Reactions to Trauma with a Special Look at PTSD

Mary

Mary had not intended to take that road, but the sign said detour, so with a sigh she turned onto an unfamiliar way home. It was dark, rainy and she just wanted to get back to her home. The windshield suddenly got filled with light, and she never even realized it was an 18 wheeler, also on the detour, who had crossed the line, and there was no place to go. The next memory was having someone looking in the window saying, "Don't move, help is on the way". The feeling of something warm dripping down her face, into her mouth seemed odd. Time didn't make sense, and nothing felt real. How could this have happened? As the months went by, the injuries healed some, but the haunting memories didn't leave. "I could have died!"

Miguel

It was a hot, horrible day. I was so tired I couldn't think. I was riding in the Humvee with Joe sitting next to me, John and Pete behind. The radio was all static. The next thing I remember is a huge, impossible explosion, and we were flying in the air! When I next looked up, we were taking fire. My head was reeling. My ears were ringing, and things just didn't look right. Then I saw Joe. Or what was left of him. His head was funny looking, it didn't look like him, and blood was everywhere. I tried to reach for him, but my left arm wouldn't move. I looked down and saw that I was bleeding too! My arm felt dead. I knew I'd never get out of here, and Joe was gone. I yelled for help, and heard Pete say you got to get out and get cover! My legs worked, and

I crawled out, pulling myself with my one good arm and pushing as best as I could with my legs. Smoke was black and hard to see through. The smell was terrible. Time stood still, and nothing looked real. Next thing I recall, I was back at the hospital. I couldn't believe it! And Joe was there, and he looked ok. It turned out he got a concussion, and had bled a lot, but he was ok. My arm had been broken, but once they fixed it up, I was going to be as good as new. Amazing.

For some, a tragedy, or trauma, can lead to a disorder called Posttraumatic Stress Disorder, or PTSD. PTSD is an anxiety disorder that has been around for as long as recorded history. Accounts of PTSD are found in early Greek literature, the aftermath of the great fire of London, and for every war that has occurred. As long as there have been human beings, we have documented the aftermath of horror and psychological anguish for some of those who survived a traumatic event.

Symptoms can be terrifying. They can impact every part of your life.

According to the National Center for Posttraumatic Stress Disorder, PTSD is an anxiety disorder that can occur after you've suffered a traumatic event. A traumatic event is something that is horrible and scary that you see or that happens to you. During the event you think that your life or the lives of others are in danger. You feel afraid or feel that you have no control over what is influencing your reaction.

Psychologists have studied and treated PTSD and the aftermath of trauma for over a hundred years. As you'll learn in this book, even the earliest treatments such as those developed by Freud, Janet and Charcot shared several important ideas with those used currently. Over time, treatments have shifted tremendously in what is focused on and what has been shown in scientific studies to be most helpful.

The four major symptom clusters for PTSD fall into the following categories:

1) A traumatic event; 2) Reexperiencing the event; 3) Avoidance of the event and/or emotional numbing (another type of avoidance of strong emotions); and 4) Symptoms of increased physical arousal. A complete list of the symptoms can be found later within this chapter.

What does PTSD look like?

As we said, there are four main groups of symptoms. Depending upon how they're put together, in theory there are over 1,750 possible combinations of these symptoms that could lead to a diagnosis of PTSD. So clearly, even though all those possible combinations are unlikely to occur in the same frequency and while we call them all PTSD, it doesn't mean it's the same experience for all people. Much like depression or anxiety, which can also be experienced as very different for people who share the label of being depressed or anxious, PTSD is not experienced the same by everyone.

But let's take a few moments to look at the major clusters. The four symptom clusters in detail are as follow:

The Traumatic Event

PTSD follows a traumatic event. Traumatic events can affect anyone. Many of our "strongest people", soldiers, policemen, and firemen, have found that in certain circumstances, anyone can develop this disorder. Traumas can include wars, sexual abuse, physical abuse, sexual or physical assault, serious accidents such as car accidents or falls, and natural disasters such as hurricanes, earthquakes, floods or tornadoes. As far as we know **no one** is so strong, so smart, and so tough that it isn't possible for this disorder to impact each and every one of us if the circumstances are just right.

To reach the level that might lead one to develop PTSD, the trauma has to be an event that would cause almost anyone to have an intense reaction. Losses such as the death of a pet can lead many of us to get quite upset. Hearing about someone suffering a tragedy can make some people worried and upset. These "lesser events" can, in fact, result in emotional problems other than PTSD. Professionals have described reactions to these events most often with other labels such as adjustment disorders, trying to describe not just the length of time but also the severity of the event that has occurred. Many people will experience psychological problems such as an adjustment disorder as a result of difficult life events such as divorce, loss of a parent, or other common difficult life events. This question about what events are serious enough to be called a true trauma and lead to PTSD has been the matter of continued debate among professionals. We won't do more here other than raise the issue and simply say that trauma is a very serious event, as Webster points out, that has a powerful impact on the people who have to deal with these tragic events.

A second reaction that is looked at when professionals are trying to determine if an event is the type of event that is appropriate for the diagnosis, is if the person's response to the event included intense fear, helplessness or horror. There is a great deal of debate about this reaction and if it really is needed to meet the criterion for PTSD, as many of our strongest individuals, warriors, police officers, and such, often don't report any of those responses, yet they too can develop the disorder. So, for our purposes, it is important to understand that the event is powerful; both in its magnitude and in an individual, as many of today's experts are defining the disorder.

Reexperiencing

This group of symptoms describes how a traumatic event plays out again and again for the individual in the period of time AFTER the event has happened. The horror won't leave. Things around you remind you that this trauma occurred. Nightmares can keep you from finding rest even in sleep. Movies, conversations, people and events that are tied to the event in your mind become associated with the terror, and can make it play over and over in your mind. It may even lead to strong physical reactions, such as a racing heart, muscle tension, or shakiness. Full-blown flashbacks, where it may seem as if you are right back there at the trauma may happen. This is like a nightmare, but while you're awake. This is what we mean by reexperiencing symptoms. Reexperiencing can get to the point where at its worst (and this is rare), you can't distinguish your surroundings or what is real. The event won't leave you alone; it fills your thoughts, your feelings, your actions, and your world.

Avoidance & Numbing

Quite understandably, people may try to avoid anything that will bring back the horrible memories or feelings tied to the trauma. You may try to not think about the event or memories, you may avoid certain people or places for fear they will trigger the reaction, and you may even be unable to recall parts of the event that others feel you should. This is a "normal reaction". No one wants these terrible thoughts or feelings to be there.

Anyone who is haunted by reminders of a horrific event, an event that leads to terrible anxiety and strong reminders of a tragic event or loss, would naturally want to avoid it. That is the crux of what occurs in this symptom cluster. A person with PTSD will make efforts to avoid thoughts, feelings, activities, events, or anything else that might remind them of the trauma. Avoidance, besides physically averting or not going to certain places or seeing certain people, may even mean amnesia, an inability to remember the event created by the person's mind in an effort to help them avoid having to face the awful feelings associated with the event.

A major part of avoidance is the avoidance of feelings. This is sometimes experienced as "numbing" of oneself. You may find it hard to feel like you did before the trauma. Things may no longer hold any interest for you, you may not feel the same positive feelings or love that should still be there for important people in your life. It's like those feelings are just turned off. All your energy is tied up in keeping the feelings and thoughts at bay, leaving little to attach to or engage in the life that you want and used to have.

The future may also look different to someone with PTSD, as if something is changed, and people with PTSD can carry a sense that they will not live as long as they once expected. This is also a change that can follow a terrible trauma.

Increased Arousal

When someone has PTSD, another change that the person may experience is in how they feel physically. There may be signs of what is called "Hyperarousal". Your nervous system is revved up. You may find it hard to sleep, find yourself losing your temper more easily than ever, your concentration may drop, and you may feel jumpy or always on the lookout, particularly for dangerous situations or potentially risky encounters.

DSM-IV PTSD Symptoms/Criteria

A complete "official listing" from the Diagnostic and Statistical Manual (4th edition) is included for your use.

Criterion A: The Traumatic Event
The person has been exposed to a traumatic event in which both of the following were present:

(1) the person experienced, witnessed, or was confronted with an event or events that involved actual or threatened death or serious injury, or a threat to the physical integrity of self or others
(2) the person's response involved intense fear, helplessness, or horror. Note: In children, this may be expressed instead by disorganized or agitated behavior

Criterion B: Persistent Reexperiencing (at least 1 of the following symptoms in this group is needed for a diagnosis)

(1) recurrent and intrusive distressing recollections of the event, including images, thoughts, or perceptions.
(2) recurrent distressing dreams of the event.
(3) acting or feeling as if the traumatic event were recurring (includes a sense of reliving the experience, illusions, hallucinations, and dissociative flashback episodes, including those that occur upon awakening or when intoxicated.
(4) intense psychological distress at exposure to internal or external cures that symbolize or resemble an aspect of the traumatic event,
(5) physiological reactivity on exposure to internal or external cues that symbolize or resemble an aspect of the traumatic event.

Criterion C: Persistent avoidance of stimuli associated with the trauma and numbing of general responsiveness (at least 3 of the following symptoms in this group are needed to have a diagnosis)

(1) efforts to avoid thoughts, feelings, or conversations associated with the trauma
(2) efforts to avoid activities, places, or people that arouse recollections of the trauma

(We divided this into the avoidance/numbing cluster in the chapter)

(3) inability to recall an important aspect of the trauma
(4) markedly diminished interest or participation in significant activities
(5) feeling of detachment or estrangement from others
(6) restricted range of affect
(7) sense of foreshortened future

Criterion D: Persistent symptoms of increased arousal (at least 2 of the following symptoms in this group are needed to have a diagnosis)

(1) difficulty falling or staying asleep
(2) irritability or outbursts of anger
(3) difficulty concentrating
(4) hypervigilance
(5) exaggerated startle response

There are a number of excellent books to help people with PTSD. These books specifically address the symptoms of PTSD and are based on our best psychological knowledge to date. A selection of these are listed at the back of the book. This book, while including information that may help people with PTSD, is instead attempting to provide an overall approach to what we know about reactions following trauma, and how to help all of us, those with and without PTSD, who have experienced a traumatic event or tragedy.

Other Reactions Besides PTSD

It is important to be clear that PTSD is not the only, and in fact is not even the most common reaction that can follow a trauma. Common reactions following a traumatic event can include fear, anxiety, sadness, anger and guilt (among others). Additionally, physical symptoms, headaches, stomach upset, sleep problems, relationship problems, and substance use can all occur. We are discussing PTSD in detail here as it is one of the most studied problems that can follow trauma, and are hoping to learn from those studies and that reaction.

My Own Experience

I don't think I developed PTSD from my fall. I say this fully sharing that when I think about the fall, I "shudder" on the inside, and still find it hard to watch a movie where someone falls and hits the ground. I can do it. However, I don't like to do it.

Most of my life I have tried to learn all I can about what is going on so I do not just understand it, but also try to know what is going to happen next. I didn't do that during my hospitalization, or even during my rehabilitation. Instead, I simply put my energy into trying to deal in the moment with what was going on around me. I fully expected to not survive the stay in the hospital, or if I did, that something awful was going to follow me out of there, either a permanent injury or disability. I didn't spend a lot of time talking about the event, but I did spend considerable time lying in the hospital bed, thinking about the event, and how I want to live now.

Mary's story continued...

As we learned at the start of this chapter, Mary couldn't shake the idea that she could have died, and the efforts to avoid the things that would remind her of her accident took up a big part of her day. She would avoid watching the news on TV for fear there might be a car accident that would make her remember her own accident. She didn't go out with friends, making up excuses that she'd rather stay home. When she rode with her husband in the car, she would often clutch the seat as he drove, and at times would yell at him for driving too fast or for not being careful enough. Finally, he just had it. In the middle of one of their fights he yelled, "I want my old Mary back!" Mary broke down crying and knew it was time to get help. But where? How?

2b: Self Assessment of Trauma & PTSD

There are only two mistakes one can make along the road to truth; not going all the way and not starting.

- Buddha

Some people find it helpful to be able to take a look at how they compare on the topics reviewed in this chapter. For that reason I have included a standard measure of life's traumas and a self report measure of PTSD.

The Traumatic Event Questionnaire (TEQ)

The TEQ is drawn from the work of Vrana & Lauterbach in the early 1990's. One important fact that we all need to keep in mind, is that life often includes more than just one traumatic event that occurs to someone. This questionnaire is a simple way to identify possible events that have had a lasting impact on your life. There is also a place for you to list an event that wasn't included in the rather complete list provided.

As you'll notice traumatic events are described in three ways; those you personally experienced, those you directly witnessed, and those you learned about from someone else. Traumas can occur in each of these ways.

The important use of the scale is to help you identify those traumas that have occurred in your life, and to help guide you in using the next questionnaire to see if any of the traumatic events MAY have resulted in you experiencing a posttraumatic stress reaction.

The TEQ is listed on the following page. If you would like to use it again, it may be useful to either copy the page, or to just use it to help identify events that have occurred in your life that might have been traumatic.

Traumatic Event Questionnaire (TEQ)

Below are a number of traumatic life events which people sometimes experience. Please read over this list carefully, and check those events that describe a significant event that you have experienced. By significant event, we are referring to events which resulted in *considerable emotional distress at the time* **and may** *continue to result in ongoing distress*. The event may have happened to you, or may have been something you witnessed.

1. Natural Disaster (e.g., flood, hurricane, earthquake) _____
2. Car accident _____
3. Plane crash _____
4. Drowning or near drowning _____
5. Machinery accident _____
6. Explosion _____
7. Home fire _____
8. Chemical Leak or exposure to radiation _____
9. Warfare or combat _____
10. Sudden AND unexpected death of someone close to you _____
11. Life threatening illness _____
12. Threatened with a weapon _____
13. Physical attack (kicked, punched, beaten up) when you were under age 18 _____
14. Physical attack (kicked, punched, beaten up) when you were over age 18 _____
15. Seeing someone killed _____
16. Someone threatening to seriously harm or kill you _____
17. Sexual abuse, sexual assault, or rape when you were under age 18 _____
18. Sexual abuse, sexual assault, or rape when you were over age 18 _____
19. Other traumatic event not yet mentioned (Please describe): _____

- Adapted from Vrana, S.R. & Lauerbach, D. (1994)

The Posttraumatic Stress Disorder Checklist (PCL)

The Posttraumatic Stress Disorder Checklist (PCL) was developed by psychologists at the National Center for PTSD, and has been used for a number of years as a way for individuals to describe the symptoms they are experiencing following a traumatic event. As you'll notice from Chapter 2, the scale lists all 17 of the symptoms of PTSD, and asks you to rate them. A total score is then obtained, as well as a way of looking at the clusters we discussed for each symptom group (reexperiencing, avoidance/numbing, and hyperarousal). These correspond to the first five items (Criterion B: items 1-5), the next seven items (Criterion C: items 6-12), and the last five items (Criterion D: items 13-17). The symptoms must be present 30 days after the event, and significantly impact your work, social or personal life.

Scores can vary depending upon the group being compared. For returning veterans seeking psychological treatment, a score of 50 is often used to identify if PTSD is present; for people who have had a car crash, a score of 44 has been used; for people in a primary care clinic, a score of 28 is sometimes used to decide to have people screened to see if they in fact have the disorder.

Remember, these are self-report instruments. While they are used in professional settings, a psychological diagnosis should be made by a trained mental health or medical professional. If the score is high, you may want to consider seeking appropriate evaluation and treatment. If it is low, it doesn't mean that even a few symptoms couldn't be extremely disturbing (e.g. nightmares) and you could still find great benefit from seeking care.

The PCL is found on the following page. Again, you may wish to copy the page, or simply take note of how you are feeling now, in case you wish to repeat the items in the future.

Posttraumatic Stress Disorder Checklist (PCL-C)

INSTRUCTIONS: Below is a list of problems and complaints that people sometimes have in response to stressful life experiences. Please read each one carefully, then rate how much how much you have been bothered by that problem *in the past month* (1=not at all, 2= a little bit, 3=moderately, 4=quite a bit, 5=extremely).

1. Repeated, disturbing *memories, thoughts*, or *images* of a stressful experience from the past? _____
2. Repeated, disturbing *dreams* of a stressful experience from the past? _____
3. Suddenly *acting* or *feeling* as if a stressful experience *were happening again* (as if you were reliving it)? _____
4. Feeling *very upset* when *something reminded you* of a stressful experience from the past? _____
5. Having *physical reactions* (e.g., heart pounding, trouble breathing, sweating) when *something reminded you* of a stressful experience from the past? _____
6. Avoiding *thinking about* or *talking about* a stressful experience from the past or avoiding *having feelings* related to it? _____
7. Avoiding *activities* or *situations* because *they reminded you* of a stressful experience from the past? _____
8. Trouble *remembering important parts* of a stressful experience from the past? _____
9. *Loss of interest* in activities that you used to enjoy? _____
10. Feeling *distant* or *cut off* from other people? _____
11. Feeling *emotionally numb* or being unable to have loving feelings for those close to you? _____
12. Feeling as if your *future* will somehow be *cut short*? _____
13. Trouble *falling* or *staying asleep*? _____
14. Feeling *irritable* or having *angry outbursts*? _____
15. Having *difficulty concentrating*? _____
16. Being *"super-alert"* or watchful or on guard? _____
17. Feeling *jumpy* or easily startled? _____

- Adapted from the PCL-C for DSM-IV (11/1/94) Weathers, Litz, Huska, & Keane National Center for PTSD - Behavioral Science Division

We grieve that Jane's away.
I know she's dead—but Gus is
Never so sure. Today
  He mopes and fusses,

And when we're back from walking
He sniffs at her armchair
And listens for her talking,
  And climbs the stair

To poke an inquiring nose
Under the hamper's lid,
For Jane, he must suppose,
  Returned and hid.

- Donald Hall, *"Searching"*

CHAPTER THREE

Why is there PTSD? How is it Treated?

Jenny

Jenny couldn't stop the thoughts of the rape from returning. No matter how she tried, the images, the fear, the memories would wash over her. She tried drinking, sometimes to the point of just passing out, and she tried asking her family doctor for sleep medicine, without saying why it was she couldn't sleep. But nothing helped. No matter where she went, however she tried to distract herself, the thoughts and feelings followed. There didn't seem to be any way out. What could possibly help?

Carlos

Carlos had been deployed 4 times. He was an Army Ranger. The best. The strongest. He had seen action in both Iraq and Afghanistan. Carlos had seen a lot. More than he would ever tell anyone. He finally came into my office when he just couldn't carry anymore. Sleep was disturbed. Images of lost friends, smells that wouldn't leave his head were with him everyday. It wasn't until he woke up looking for a weapon and he'd accidently hit his pregnant wife that he knew it had to stop. He'd thought of suicide. It seemed to make sense. But he had a wife and soon a baby. Who would take care of them? That was the day he first came to see me for help, to see what we could do together to change the way he was feeling and how he could get the life he most wanted.

Now that you've learned what PTSD looks like, I'd like to discuss briefly what psychologists think about why PTSD develops. For professionals it's important to have some idea about what leads to a disorder, so treatments can be designed that address those reasons. If as a patient, we understand why something is done, it makes it much more likely that we'll be willing to follow those steps, even if they seem counter intuitive, and not what one would want to do at first.

That's what this chapter is about: to share briefly some of the current psychological theories of PTSD and to describe some of the major elements in treatments that research has found to be most successful. This will be our first step into sharing what can be of help in transforming your trauma. Learning from our best treatments to date is a good place to begin. In the next few chapters, I'll also share what doesn't help, and what puts some people at greater risk for staying stuck with their suffering and not getting past their traumas.

Several treatment approaches have been scientifically shown to help people dealing with PTSD. A list of the major sources are offered at the end of the book and interested readers who want to know more are encouraged to read them for more details and depth.

What I would like to do here is to show what has been done in the treatment of PTSD that has been successful, to learn how this might help all of us move through life's tragedies a little more effectively, and to benefit from the lessons learned in dealing with this adverse reaction to a traumatic event.

Why PTSD?

This may seem like an unusual question, but given the number of traumas that happen, and the variety of reactions that can follow, why would anyone develop PTSD is a pretty important question. Why is it many people don't develop PTSD, even when they went through horrible experiences, while others develop PTSD following what seems like little contact, and at least on the outside they look fine? Why don't we have the ability to just "deal with it"? Why do we instead develop such a powerful disorder that gives us so much pain and suffering?

The real answer, at least at this time, is no one truly knows. There are a number of theories, and some evidence for each of those theories. My personal answer, that comes after considerable thought and experience, is that part of being human quite naturally leads to suffering. We think. We feel. We understand. We learn. We remember. We develop PTSD.

Doesn't it make sense that if something bad hurts us we will reflect on it, remember it, and try to avoid it in the future? We want to be safe, we want to avoid pain, and we want to stay alive. We also think about things. We make up associations. This happens automatically, we don't have to think. If we were in a car accident, we associate cars after our injury as a place of possible pain. The same is true for other traumas or tragedies. It's natural to do this. We also think about what things mean. We understand we will someday die, or we can be injured so badly we will lose our life as we know it. It is right to try to do anything we can to protect ourselves and stay safe. And that thinking, that trying to find understanding, for most of us leads to dramatic psychological reactions and consequences.

So, with this in mind let's briefly look at what some of the leading theorists in psychology believe leads someone to develop PTSD.

Theory Number 1 - The Two Factor Theory (Mowrer 1947; Keane et al 1985)

In this theory we see the reexperiencing symptoms following trauma as a normal reaction. You are trying to make sense of what is going through your mind. It doesn't mean you're going crazy, or "losing your mind". Almost everyone has something like this type of remembering and reliving moments of the trauma. Unfortunately, it is easy to also develop a ***fearful response***, which can become tied to the event. This can be from a car accident where you just learned that it is dangerous out there, and the memories and reactions from the accident are instantly tied to previously normal events like driving, or watching the news that now generate anxiety or uncomfortable feelings when they occur. This means a lot of things, thoughts, symbols, activities, feelings that used to be "normal" are now tied to the event, and a ***fearful response is conditioned or associated by this learning!*** Now one can have a strong reaction seemingly "out of the blue".

The second factor is that the ***avoidance response furthers this learning.*** As we said, it's normal to want to avoid situations, feelings or thoughts that make us feel bad. But now add in this learned response that has us avoiding these feelings each time we are confronted by them. As you may know or imagine, this avoidance buys you a temporary relief from the unpleasant reaction, which then feels positive and understandable, for a little while at least. As this happens, it strengthens the likelihood you'll continue to use these avoidance techniques, which only serves to strengthen the reaction. This theory then suggests that the avoidance stops anyone from facing and mastering the unpleasant reactions, and in fact the avoidance contributes to the development of the disorder. This is especially true, as the things that result in these feelings are inescapable, and therefore can't fully be avoided; they are your normal life, your own feelings, and your own memories and thoughts.

To show this within the two factor theory:

Factor 1: Trauma leads to fearful, scary, anxious reactions and memories that are linked to normal things in life.

Factor 2: As feelings from trauma are linked to places, thoughts, feelings, they lead to avoidance; The avoidance, which brings temporary relief in order to try to decrease the fear, then strengthens the avoidance reaction each time we avoid.

Just to illustrate how hard it is to avoid some things, that the suppression of thoughts for example is extremely difficult, let's try a little experiment.

Let's try NOT to think about something. We can pick something really silly, like an elephant. Like a little baby elephant.

For the next 60 seconds try, NOT TO THINK ABOUT ELEPHANTS..........ANY KIND OF ELEPHANTS...PINK, BLUE, GRAY, BIG, SMALL, ANY KIND OF ELEPHANT. Try not to think about elephants.

Start now.............

So, how'd you do? Not so well? Even if you change the thought to horses, or dogs, or numbers, you still know in the back of your mind what you're really trying to do. It is just the way the mind works to not allow us to suppress or hold back an idea like that. So, when the thought is not a silly thought, but a very powerful, deeply frightening or even horrible thought, it becomes even harder. The mind is forcing the replaying of the memory. The same concept is applied to feelings (anxiety), and behaviors (not driving after a crash, or going to the scene of the assault). This avoidance can generalize to other places, (any dark place, any similar place with people, etc.), and pretty soon our world is shrinking.

Theory Number 2 - Emotion Processing- Fear Network (Lang, 1977, 1979; Foa 1989)

Another theory believes that memories are tied to the trauma, and this results in a large number of fears becoming tied to cues, associations and emotions linked to the trauma. This theory builds on the two factor theory (remember first we get a scared reaction (factor 1) and then we avoid, which strengthens the fear (factor 2), and looks more closely at how our thoughts and reactions lead to PTSD.

A fear network is a number of memories directly related to the trauma (including sights, smells, reactions and meanings) that become tied to a number of other elements (thoughts, behaviors, etc.) many of which are actually mistakes and not very well organized or thought out. The theory states that the problem is that the trauma has never been fully "processed", so the person remembers it in intense bits and pieces that lead to fear and to mistakes about the meaning of the trauma. Because of these features, this fear memory network is easily activated in individuals with PTSD. When it is activated, it causes individuals with PTSD to respond behaviorally, physiologically, emotionally, and cognitively as if they are back in the traumatic event, demonstrating impairment in emotional processing of the trauma and accounting for the symptoms of PTSD.

Again, individuals with PTSD use active avoidance strategies and emotional numbing, and these strategies serve to prevent memory activation sufficient for successful emotional processing of the trauma memories. If you never get to feel a large portion of the horror again, it becomes impossible to change any incorrect or dysfunctional ways of looking at past, present or future situations within that network of things that lead to the fearful reaction. Ideas can be anything, thoughts such as "the world is very dangerous", "I have no control over anything", "I can't tolerate the painful emotions related to my trauma". This then prevents anyone "habituating" (staying in the painful situation long enough so that the reactions can grow less, and no longer evoke such frightening memories). If the fear network remains unchanged, PTSD symptoms will persist.

How does theory lead to treatment?

To facilitate emotional processing during therapy, trauma survivors are asked to try to relive the trauma memory repeatedly to fully activate the fear network. This provides a chance to habituate (get a less and less strong response) to the trauma memory they are reliving/recalling. Treatment, especially those which see beliefs as important, also attempts to correct any "erroneous beliefs" ("I can't handle the emotional pain", "I'll never get better", "If it happens again, I'll die") that drive avoidance of the trauma memory and contribute to avoidant behaviors (e.g. not thinking about the trauma, not acting in certain ways).

So, major elements of treatment are repeated thinking, talking and doing things that activate the feelings, and staying there long enough to not have the same reactions. This is combined with trying to discover what thoughts might be leading to beliefs about the person, the world or the future that might be contributing to the avoidant behaviors and substituting more accurate, or rational thoughts.

Theory Number 3 - Cognitive Processing (Ehlers & Clark, 2000; Resick & Schnicke, 1993)

This psychological theory emphasizes that what is most important is how we think about the trauma, which then determines if we ultimately develop PTSD. If the traumatic event is processed (thought about) in such a way that it now results in the person seeing threat in situations that are not necessarily threatening (such as returning to the scene of the trauma when it's now actually safe; TV shows that stir up feelings that they believe will be overwhelming), the PTSD symptoms (reexperiencing, arousal, anxiety, anger) will result. This theory argues it is important how one views the trauma (e.g. the belief that these reactions will lessen over time and the fear will pass versus the belief that these fears and other reactions will be long lasting if not forever). These trauma researchers argue that since the trauma memories are typically not very well organized ("I can't keep the details straight, they are all fragments, mixed up, with gaping holes at times"), unlike most of our memories which are more defined (like who we are - "I'm a man, with these parents"); where we come from ("Born in this city, grew up here, live in this place", etc.) the symptoms result in actions and thoughts that are largely to be avoided or escaped because of the uncomfortable feelings and the distress the memories and intrusive thoughts can cause.

Individuals who see the trauma and its reactions/impact as a time-restricted event that does not inevitably lead to long lasting bad effects, will typically recover more quickly than those who have excessively negative beliefs and views of the event and believe that they can't get over it. These individual differences in the memory of the event determine if a sense of current threat is activated, along with all those PTSD symptoms. Remember, it is normal to have strong reactions when confronted with an actual threat; PTSD is a condition where those reactions continue even at times when there is no threat present. It is argued that the nature of the trauma memory is different from other autobiographical memories (i.e. things that have happened to a person) in that trauma memories are not well organized, but can still be extremely vivid and powerful. In contrast, other autobiographical memories, both concrete and abstract, are well organized (e.g. by themes, personal time periods, etc.), which makes retrieving them easy and natural. This lack of organization of the trauma memory stops or limits the activation of the intense emotional re-experiencing of the trauma, thereby interfering with the habituation to the trauma memory (i.e. experiencing less and less anxiety as you remember the trauma and no bad consequence actually happens). Just as an experiment, let's try a simple association as a type of "mind test".

Without thinking about it, insert the first word that comes to mind:

Twinkle, twinkle, little __________.

For the majority of us, we probably said "star". It's automatic, over-learned, and requires no thought. Like Coke is the real ______. (Thing! What does that even mean?)

Now, as the second part to the experiment, let's try to think anything BUT star for the Twinkle, twinkle phrase. Ready?

Twinkle, twinkle little ________.

How'd you do? Maybe with a lot of effort you were able to force (temporarily) a new word. But wasn't there a part of your mind that needed to be caught up thinking, "not STAR"? That's the way our minds work. It's automatic. Over learned. We can't force ourselves to be anything other than what we are. Thoughts, feelings, associations are normal. I sometimes use the association of walking by a bakery and smelling bread or cookies baking. The smells, at least for me, often make me smile, and even make me feel happy. Why? What is so powerful about bread baking? Nothing, by itself, BUT THE ASSOCIATIONS formed over my life, memories of my mother giving me a piece of freshly baked, buttered bread in a warm, cozy kitchen, is an old, comfortable memory. The same type of blending happens with bad memories. Just ask any combat veteran if they have any smells that stir up bad memories or reactions. It's normal. It's powerful. No one asks for "star" to show up. It just does. It's what we do next that will show us a way out of the pain.

So, to Sum Up

First, behavioral or cognitive avoidance strategies may lead directly to an increase in PTSD symptoms. For example, thought suppression (i.e. pushing thoughts out of mind) has the paradoxical effect of increasing intrusions. In other words, trying to avoid thinking about something actually makes you think about it more.

Second, maladaptive behaviors may indirectly contribute to the continuance of the disorder by thwarting alteration of the negative views and reactions (e.g. checking and safety behaviors temporarily reduce anxiety, and thereby avert the predicted/expected negative consequences of engaging in more adaptive behaviors like resuming your prior way of life). In other words, the more you do to try to get rid of the anxious feelings by avoiding people, places or things that remind you of the trauma, the longer those feelings will hang around in your life.

Third, maladaptive behavioral and/or cognitive strategies are employed preventing changes in the nature of the trauma memory itself. These strategies include tactics such as "trying not to think" about the event by either consuming oneself in distracting thoughts or engaging in behaviors to divert attention from the trauma memories. In other words, avoiding remembering the traumatic event from beginning to end keeps you from understanding what really happened to you and how to deal effectively with the memories of the trauma.

What have we learned?

Avoidance, memories, and thoughts all are important to how we currently see the development and continuation of PTSD. These same elements are tied to how we think about doing treatment. With this in mind, we are on our path to learning how to transform the way we deal with the aftermath of our own trauma.

Macbeth and PTSD?

Macbeth: Canst though not minister to a mind diseased, Pluck from the memory a rooted sorrow, Raze out the written troubles of a brain, and with some sweet, oblivious antidote, Cleanse the stuff'd bosom of that perilous stuff, Which weighs upon the heart?

Doctor: Therein the patient must minister to himself.

- William Shakespeare, "Macbeth"

3b: The Center for Stress and Anxiety Disorders

PTSD Treatment Studies

My first job out of graduate school was working at the Samuel Stratton VA in Albany, NY as a consultation liaison psychologist. That meant I was the mental health professional who was sent around the hospital helping medical staff deal with the psychological problems and disorders that occurred while they were treating the physical problems that brought veterans to the hospital. I spent a lot of time on the floors seeing patients, speaking with staff, and trying to respond to consult requests to help patients and staff deal with psychological concerns. I liked the job a lot and had the privilege to work with a number of our combat veterans from the Vietnam War. In addition to helping them deal with their physical problems such as coping with heart disease, cancer, or neurological illness, I helped them with their PTSD, depression and anxiety as part of that treatment team. It was hard, but incredibly rewarding work.

When I left the VA to enter a full time practice, I brought those experiences and that knowledge with me. And, after a while, I thought I began to see in some of my patients what looked like PTSD following car crashes. But, in those days, in order to have PTSD, the trauma had to be "outside the range of normal human activities". Remember when we talked earlier about the issue of what exactly is a trauma? Well, that question followed me to my office, and over to a colleague and friend at the University at Albany, Dr. Edward Blanchard. After we saw that very little had been written about how to understand and help car crash survivors, we had an idea that led to nearly 20 years of clinical research. We began looking at the psychological impact of car crashes, and saw that PTSD in fact was there as well as in combat veterans and rape survivors. At that time, there weren't any active wars, and we found in this group of trauma survivors, a group of people who were willing to share their stories with us, and to allow us to study their reactions, and eventually to try our ideas of how to help them.

This chapter uses that story to summarize some of the key elements of what goes into a psychological treatment to illustrate how these theories are put into place.

The Albany MVA Project

The Albany Motor Vehicle Accident (MVA) Project grew out of an interest in looking at traumatic events that can result in PTSD or other significant psychological reactions. We saw MVA-related trauma as a model for how trauma can lead to psychological distress that could possibly be applied to other types of traumatic events. MVAs occurred with a great deal of frequency, the people involved were willing to talk about their trauma, and unlike other traumas such as rape or sexual assault, the people involved were often agreeable to be followed and studied for years, even if they didn't receive any formal treatment. The other fortunate fact of MVAs was that a great number of people did not develop significant psychological problems, and this allowed for comparisons to try to see what led to distress in some people, and not in others. MVAs, as it turns out, are the most common traumatic event that happens to people in developed westernized countries.

Once we gained skill in assessing the problems that result from this trauma, we wanted to help the people we had studied. The first thing we did was to look at each cluster of symptoms (like you learned about in Chapters 2) and then we used what we believed were the most effective psychological treatments available at the time to deal with them. This brings us back to that list of symptom clusters; reexperiencing, avoidance/numbing and hyperarousal. Each had to be addressed in a treatment. Here's how we did it.

Reexperiencing

Reexperiencing, as you've learned, is at the heart of posttraumatic reactions. The thoughts of what happened to you intrude into daily life and the memories of what happened, including feelings, fears, and images that won't leave you alone. Not even in sleep is there any rest for sufferers of this disorder because of distressing dreams. Reminders of the trauma are everywhere, as so many parts of our life are often touched by the impact of the traumatic event. So what do psychologists do to help? Tell someone not to think about it? That really doesn't work so well, as you learned with the elephant experiment. Instead, as each of the theories we discussed suggests, the opposite is needed, to face that which one prefers to avoid.

This confrontation of feared events, thoughts and feelings has turned out to be a very powerful part of many psychological treatments, and is termed **exposure therapy**. Exposure therapy involves facing the feared event in a way that allows it to be changed into a less provocative event, an event that can be better managed and carried.

One way this is done is that when the memories are brought up in a therapeutic setting, they are dealt with differently than when the memories come up in other parts of one's life. First off there is a therapist. That person is supportive, doesn't get scared with whatever the reaction is, has an understanding of what is happening and why, and has joined the person on their journey to get better.

Second, the actual traumatic event is no longer present or occurring; it has happened in the past and is now internal to the survivor. In therapy, there is a focus on the difference between the TRAUMA and the MEMORIES of the trauma. The forces that are being dealt with are the ones inside the person, namely their memories, their feelings, and their subsequent behaviors. These are being dealt with in a manner that allows the person to begin to separate the past trauma from the current reaction, and their fears of what will happen next.

Third, when you think of something scary over and over in detail, what happens? It loses its impact. Think of the scariest movie you ever saw. Think of the scariest scene. Now remember your first reaction to that scene. Then imagine having a copy of the movie, and playing just that scene over and over again and again, 100 times, maybe even 200 times. Now how strong would your reaction be? Probably a lot less than the first time you saw the scary scene. Maybe you would have very little reaction at all. That is exposure. That is what was meant in the earlier chapter by the term, habituation.

This approach in treatment helps a trauma survivor access the feelings and thoughts about the trauma and then confront those things that up to this point had caused such a very powerful reaction. That powerful reaction is what drives the person away from the ideas or memories that are difficult to deal with, to avoid them. The exposure treatments help make these memories conscious, and ultimately to generate much less intense negative reactions, resulting in less avoidance.

As you've learned, one well accepted model of what perpetuates PTSD and keeps it so powerful, is that the avoidance of the very strong, negative reactions that come from the memories and this avoidance is what makes it impossible to ever resolve and find a way to deal with the memories.

We run from the memories because they feel so awful. By running away from the memories and feelings, we never find a way to understand what is driving them, and how to carry those ideas and memories with us through our lives in a different way.

Avoidance

How did we help someone change this set of symptoms?

The first step was helping people understand how avoidance, while a normal reaction, can actually worsen the symptoms as we explained in the last chapter.

The second step was to teach a set of skills that could help people deal with the feelings that often come up when they stop avoiding those things that were causing the powerful memories of the trauma. These skills include ways to deal with thoughts and feelings using cognitive behavioral techniques. These skills are going to be taught in later chapters.

The third step was to slowly introduce things (thoughts, feelings, memories, situations) that would lead to different levels of distress, and then from easiest to hardest, to begin to face them one at a time, one by one. It was important never to move on to the next step until the one they were dealing with was dealt with successfully.

Fourth, we helped people learn about the thoughts and beliefs they had that contributed to their feelings and reactions, and how to change them.

Last, as they were willing, we met with them and their significant other, to share information about reactions to trauma, including PTSD, and how treatment was designed to help those symptoms. If someone was going to make this kind of change, we believed it was going to be noticed in a relationship, and it made sense to let the people affected know what was going on and why. We also, as indicated, pointed out where the significant other, as someone who cared about the trauma survivor, might inadvertently help in the avoidance by just trying to be a caring partner. Husbands might drive their wife to the store or go themselves instead, in an effort to help their wife not feel bad. If this was to occur, we wanted them to know how the goals in treatment might also include them watching a person they love do some difficult tasks, and to be supportive, but not stop them by "being helpful".

Psychic Numbing & Estrangement

This cluster of symptoms is hard to know what to do with as a treating psychologist. There were few studies or theories to guide us here, so we had to do the best we could. The idea of trying to get someone "to feel more" is difficult to figure out. Numbing is often viewed as another type of avoidance, the avoidance of strong emotions. This is why the feelings are "turned off". Another disorder where interest and feelings are dampened is depression. Consequently, one helpful way we thought about these symptoms was to see emotional numbing as closely resembling depression.

Comparison of PTSD and Depression Symptoms

PTSD	**Depression**
-Diminished interests	-Diminished interest & pleasure
-Restricted affect	-Depressed mood
-Decreased concentration	-Diminished thinking/ concentration
-Sleep disturbance	-Insomnia/hypersomnia
-Foreshortened future	-Thoughts of death
-Irritability/anger	-Agitation / restlessness/anger
-Poor recall of trauma	-Diminished thinking/ concentration
-Hypervigilance	-Psychomotor agitation

When we saw the symptom cluster this way, we designed an intervention that used cognitive behavioral therapy, a recognized treatment for depression as well as PTSD, and also included pleasant events scheduling (PES). PES is a very old behavioral intervention that simply asks depressed people to try to do at least one thing each day (more if they can) that, in the past or potentially in the present, has the chance of giving them some pleasure. They are instructed not to wait until they feel like doing the task, but rather to do the task no matter how they feel. For depressed people, if you can get them moving and involved in doing things that have the chance of some pleasure, positive feelings often follow the action. So, the take home message was, "don't wait until you feel like doing it to do it; rather do it, and see if the positive feelings can eventually follow".

Hyperarousal

This group of symptoms involves the physical sensations that frequently are a part of the PTSD reaction. How can we quiet these? Again, there were many strategies to draw from.

First, to quiet the heightened anxiety and arousal as they occur, including increased heart rate, respirations, muscle tension and feelings of panic, one tried and true technique is relaxation training. Relaxation training has also been shown to be helpful in dealing with PTSD symptoms overall, and is a skill which most people can readily learn and apply as needed. Further, it is a tool that can help someone have the confidence to step into some of the rather scary places psychological recovery can hold.

Related to the arousal is the question, "What is it that sets off the arousal?" Are they internal cues or things in the environment? Again, how we think about things, or our cognitions, play a large role. Helping someone learn what thoughts are triggers to the arousal, or how they might contribute to the continuation of the reactions, turned out to be a large part of helping people with these particular symptoms.

What Did Treatment Look Like Overall?

Using the components described above, our treatment for PTSD following motor vehicle accidents took between 8-12 weeks, with an average of 10 weeks. Treatment began with a good explanation and introduction to what PTSD is, teaching relaxation skills, introducing the idea of exposure, and sending the person off to write about their accident. When they returned, treatment continued to include exposure to the memories of their trauma, both in session and outside, by listening as they read aloud the description of the accident with all the vivid details and memories they could remember. Each participant was taught how their thinking leads to unwanted reactions, and how thoughts contribute to the way the symptoms are continued. Then they were given a simple method to learn about these thoughts, and to challenge them in a way that could impact the way they were feeling. Pleasant events scheduling was introduced and encouraged. Relaxation skills were performed over and over, until they became over learned, and the training in relaxation skills ended with very brief ways to bring about a relaxed feeling. The latter part of treatment addressed common problems that can also be present, including depression, anger, and existential issues (i.e. facing near death, and the meaning of one's life).

How did we do?

Overall, as compared with people who had not received any treatment, or those who received supportive therapy only, 76% of the MVA survivors we treated no longer met criteria for PTSD. There was also an improvement on measures of psychological well being and overall functioning. As with the treatments introduced in earlier chapters, there is strong evidence that these psychological interventions can make a dramatic difference in how people feel.

So what should one do at this point?

This book may not solve all of the problems that you may have developed because of the traumas and tragedies in your life. That may require other help, such as a therapist or counselor. We hope it gives you as much relief as it can. However, its intent is to provide an overall view of what we do know, and ways to use that knowledge in a general way. The details of that knowledge will be offered in the chapters that follow. In the meantime, here is what we do know with some degree of certainty.

If you want to get over symptoms of PTSD, findings from our empirically validated treatments (they've been shown to work in scientific studies), suggest the following:

- **Exposure is good**. In one way or another, it is important to face those things that are most feared and avoided. Exposure requires you to stay in the situation or to stay with the memory for enough time so the fear reactions can lessen, and one can regroup with a new reaction.
- **Cognitive Restructuring**, (identifying and changing unhelpful beliefs and attitudes) works. Our thoughts greatly influence our world and our reactions to how we deal with and experience the world.
- **Relaxation in some form helps**. If one can quiet some of the storm inside, more things become possible, as well as just feeling better.
- **Confront feared situations**. Avoidance has been shown to worsen, not help, post trauma reactions. While avoidance may buy some relief for the moment, avoidance greatly increases the chance that

the symptoms won't improve and can even get worse over time.

- **Avoidance doesn't work**, both in how we try to suppress or distract ourselves from trauma related thoughts, or in avoidance of the feelings and behaviors that make up our lives.
- **Take it in manageable steps**. Too much too soon can lead to a worsening of the reaction, and increase the desire to escape and thereby avoid the negative feelings. Mastery, generally gained gradually over time, is the key, not rushing through any part of treatment.
- **You need some arousal to change**. "No pain, no gain" applies here. In order to get over this, you need to feel things you probably don't want to feel. These are some of the most uncomfortable feelings and memories one can have. The good news is that by facing and dealing with those reactions, you offer yourself a chance (but there is no guarantee, even our best treatments don't help everyone) that you will improve how you feel and return more closely to living the kind of life you'd like.
- **Identify thoughts that lead to emotional reactions**. Emotions don't come from a vacuum. There is a trigger. Most of the time there is a thought that leads to the reaction. It might be a thought about the way you're feeling something physically; it might be a thought about yourself and your future. If you can identify the thoughts, you're more than halfway there to changing their effect on you.
- **Look for cognitive distortions**. Memories of traumas are often loaded with untruths and misperceptions. So much happens so fast, that it is hard to have it make sense. It doesn't fit into an easy memory of who we are and what it means or says about us. If there are misperceptions about you ("I'm abnormal"), or

the future ("I'll never get better"), or anything else, finding a way to recognize and alter the misperception is often helpful.

- **Reminders**. The things that can remind you of what happened can be anywhere. It may be in conversations with people you love who simply ask you how you're doing. It may be in a scene in a movie that uses an image or a sound that brings it all back. It may even be a smell you had not even noticed at first, but now it's linked to the awful way you feel. Or it may be a physical injury and continuing pain or limitations that ties you and the traumatic memory into the present. Trying to avoid these reminders can lead to your world becoming smaller and smaller. How you learn to see the reminders, to respond to them, and limit the effect they have is another important part of making progress. Meeting reminders is an unavoidable part of life.

"If you don't know where you're going, any road can take you there"

- C.S. Lewis

Or by a more "modern" person,

"If you don't know where you're going you might not get there"

- Yogi Berra

Chapter Four

What Puts Someone at Risk for PTSD?
Why Me?

Martha

Mary's friend Martha had a motor vehicle accident almost a year to the day before Mary's. It was a bad crash. She had been going through an intersection when a teenage driver struck her car on the passenger's side. Martha's car was pushed through the intersection, ultimately hitting a telephone pole where it came to a stop. At first she didn't know what had happened. Fortunately she was wearing her seatbelt, and her car had side air bags, which deployed. She remembered thinking "Wow! I'm incredibly lucky to have such a good car." "I knew I bought a Volvo for a reason!" She got out of the car, and went to see the other driver. Fortunately, neither was too badly hurt, although they were taken by ambulance to the nearby hospital where Martha's husband worked.

The next few days and weeks were busy getting the car repaired, and reorganizing her schedule as a drug rep where she needed to keep driving in her region. She did have the chance to speak with her group of friends, both on the phone, and in the twice weekly walks she and her best friend had been doing for years. There had been some anxiety getting back in the car, and when she drove through the intersection she indeed felt somewhat upset for several weeks. But, it was the shortest way to take her kids to their activities, and there was no avoiding it other than taking routes that wouldn't have added considerably to her already tight schedule. They needed her, and she couldn't depend on a husband who, while he cared, was often caught up in his work. Over time thoughts of the accident became less and less, until one day she was watching TV and noticed that a really bad crash in the city simply raised her concern for the other driver, but did not cause any immediate distress related to her own crash, so many weeks before.

John

John had been in two accidents before this one. This time, he was simply trying to get off a highway ramp, and the other driver was coming right at him! He woke several minutes later, not sure where he was, or what was going on. He knew he had broken several bones, and there was blood all over the place. Someone appeared next to him and told him not to move. The EMTs were on the way. His next memory was in the ER. The doctor told him he'd been in a terrible crash and was lucky just to be alive. They were going to do everything they could to keep it that way, and he needed emergency surgery right away. His family had been contacted, and they would be there when he woke up.

The next few days and weeks were a blur. His arm was fractured and his head felt like it had gone through the ringer. Headaches, dizziness, even nausea. The pills helped some with the pain, but they made it hard to focus. He knew he couldn't drive for quite a while, and frankly didn't want to. Three accidents in a year! It's dangerous out there. And the pain! Everyday he had a reason to remember. Friends brought pictures of his smashed car, and he even saw a clip of himself being placed on a stretcher at the accident scene. He had also been told that the other driver died as a result of injuries suffered from the crash. No charges were brought against John. In fact, the authorities commended him from doing all he could to avoid the other driver. But he still felt there was more he could have done. He just couldn't get those images and the fragments of memories of what happened out of his head. He found himself falling back into depression, a place he hadn't been for several years.

Before we move on, I'd like to share some of what we know about what makes some people at greater risk for developing PTSD following a trauma than other people. As was mentioned earlier, if life wears us down enough through repeated assaults, it is believed that most of us could develop this disorder. But for some people, there does appear to be a greater risk than for others, and this information might be of use to us as we try to learn what we can do to weather our own storms as best as possible.

Some of the risk factors that are associated with the symptoms that show up following or during the traumatic event include:

- **Dissociative Symptoms:** This refers to when you feel as if you or your surroundings aren't real or what is happening is not really happening to you. You may feel out of it or as if you are watching rather than experiencing the events, or you may not even be aware of your surroundings or what you did or said during the trauma. There is evidence that people who experience dissociative symptoms at the time of the trauma are more at risk for PTSD.
- **Reexperiencing Symptoms:** The stronger and more intense the reexperiencing symptoms, the higher the risk for later problems. So, if you had frequent unwanted and intense memories of the trauma that were overwhelming for you shortly after the event or if you had intense nightmares that replayed the trauma, you may fall into this risk category.

- **Avoidance:** The more someone attempts to avoid thoughts or behaviors related to the trauma, the higher the risk for PTSD. Perhaps this is because the avoidance has the unintended effect of actually strengthening the negative feelings or perhaps it's because the intensity of the need to avoid is an indication of how much suffering is taking place. Either way, the stronger the avoidance, the higher the risk is for PTSD.
- **Physical Injuries/Pain:** Being injured in the trauma seems to increase the chance of post trauma reactions. It may be due to the fact that the pain is a reminder of what happened, or perhaps the ways that the injuries limit you and the things you can no longer do. This can negatively affect the way you see yourself now and in your future. This might also include subtle cognitive changes, such as poor concentration from a concussion that now feeds and interacts with the poor concentration from anxiety that resulted from the trauma.
- **Perceived Life Threat:** If you thought you were in danger of dying, or believed you were about to die, your risk of developing PTSD is increased. Perhaps the fear that results from a threat to one's life is so intense that it is not easily overcome, or it may be that the threat to life is a measure of the severity of the trauma itself.
- **Negative Emotions During the Trauma:** If you felt terrified, out of control, petrified with fear, or other intense negative emotions while the trauma was occurring, your risk is greater. We believe this occurs in part due to the "imprinting" or tying of emotions to memories that contribute to the powerful associations as well as the poorly organized way of remembering all that was taking place.

- **Cognitive Processing During the Trauma:** If the event is scattered, jumbled in terms of images, thoughts, with memories with "holes", the chance of PTSD is increased.

Other risk factors might be in your history. These include:

- **Prior Depression:** People with a prior history of depression are at greater risk.
- **Prior Trauma History:** The more traumas in one's life, the greater the likelihood this current one will leave adverse reactions. Rather than making us stronger, the data seems to bear out that traumas erode us; prior traumas make us more vulnerable and put us at greater risk for PTSD.
- **Being Female:** We're not yet sure why, but it seems that women are at greater risk for developing PTSD just by virtue of being female. This is somewhat surprising given that men often are in more high risk jobs and more dangerous situations. This is a complicated risk factor, compounded by cultural factors, psychological makeup, biological factors, and the types of traumas experienced (women experience more sexual trauma, men more combat exposure). In fact, when we compare both men and women who have been raped, the men are actually more likely to develop PTSD than the women.
- **Limited Family Support and/or Few Social Supports After the Trauma:** People who are on their own, alone, or with few social supports do less well following a trauma than people who have and use their social supports in the aftermath of their traumas.

Behaviors that increase the risk of PTSD:

- **Social Withdrawal:** People who hunker down, and then continue to limit their contact with the world, are at greater risk for PTSD than those who don't withdraw to the same degree. It is important to point out, however, that a good number of people need time to regroup and heal following their trauma. It is the continuation of the withdrawal that is important as a risk factor for greater risk of adverse reactions.

- **Restricted Pleasure Behavior:** If there is no laughter, no joy, and limited efforts to seek those moments out, over time, the risk for PTSD rises.
- **Safety Behaviors:** (i.e., excessive precautions such as checking and re-checking door and window locks). Safety behaviors reflect how one deals with the world after a trauma. Again, some safety behaviors are normal and positive precautions. But it is the degree, appropriateness and longevity of these behaviors that lead to concern about the lasting or continued effect of symptoms.
- **Alcohol or Drug Over-Use or Abuse:** The use of substances to "numb" feelings or avoid thoughts is a common reaction to the experience of trauma. Like other types of avoidance, it may make things feel a little better for a short time, but actually increases the likelihood of PTSD and other problems over the longer term.

Cognitions that increase the risk of PTSD:

- **Perception of Dying:** This perception and the fear that follows often greatly changes how we view ourselves and the world around us, and if present, increases the chance of PTSD.
- **Continued Negative Ways of Looking at Your Self & the World:** In keeping with our cognitive theories of PTSD, if one holds these types of appraisals, (or sizing things up through ideas and judgments), these persistent negative judgments increase the chance of PTSD.
- **Negative Appraisals of the Trauma & Sequelae:** This is similar, but now the appraisals are not about oneself and the world, but rather the trauma itself, and how it has changed everything in a negative fashion.

- **Rumination & Thought Suppression:** The presence of continued, uncontrollable thoughts and sustained efforts to control those thoughts, add to the chance that an adverse reaction including PTSD can occur.

Others factors contributing to the risk of PTSD:

- **Death:** If there was a death involved in the traumatic event, the chance of developing PTSD is increased. Obviously, events that include the loss of human life can be extremely distressing and very difficult for one to incorporate and carry.
- **Experiencing the Trauma Alone vs. with Others:** While we don't have hard data on this point, experience has suggested that if you share the trauma with others, typically friends or co-workers, it is sometimes easier to deal with trauma than if you are dealing with a tragedy that only you experienced. Firemen deal with some truly awful moments. Yet, the fraternal nature of firemen and how they share in the events they experience, seems to be extremely helpful. There is a built in support system. The same is often found in natural disasters, or events like 9/11 where people support one another, and help at a time of need.

So, as we look at the two examples that began this chapter, we see in Martha someone who did not experience terrifying thoughts or reactions at the scene of her accident. She actually was able to stay focused and looked to help the individual who ran into her car. She didn't think she was going to die. Martha's lifestyle, including having a busy family and a job that required her to drive, required her to NOT AVOID driving or those things that might have provoked unsettling feelings or memories. She didn't think she was going to die. She had friends, stayed involved socially and didn't isolate herself. She talked about the event as much as she thought appropriate with the friends she had. Her husband, while busy, was supportive. Overall, other than being female, most of the risk factors were absent for her. No lingering pain, no distorted memories of the event, no belief that she was in great danger or that she could have died.

In contrast, John had a significant trauma history with prior car accidents. He had a history of depression, which again added to his risk for PTSD, as did the following; his belief that he could have died in the accident, his poor memories of the event, the ongoing pain, and the death of the other driver. The way he interpreted the events also increased his risk; even though there was probably nothing he could have done to change it, he felt responsible for the other driver's death.

Risk factors are not anyone's fault. They just are, like a family history of some medical illnesses that may put you at greater risk than people who don't have the same history. We share them here to help see who might be at greater risk for developing PTSD. Having risk factors doesn't mean you will develop PTSD, even if you have ALL of them, but it does mean, on average, your risk will be increased.

In my own case, I was facing several of the risk factors as well. I thought on several prior occasions or during bad events that I could or was about to die or be severely injured or disabled. I was in great pain. I had moments of reliving or re-experiencing the fall and the events that followed. But, I also had a great support system. A caring family. A good number of friends that came by. They stayed with me. I didn't get ahead of myself, I tried to stay present and not see more than I could in my future. I did not avoid the feelings or thoughts, but tried to experience them as they occurred, as natural, understandable (albeit really unpleasant and frightening) occurrences. It was a time to take stock of who I was and how to act in ways that were consistent with who I wanted to be. If these were my last moments, how did I want to live them? What words did I want to say? I think those methods, and others that we'll get to in later chapters, helped me not to ruminate or get caught up in the negative spiral that could have occurred.

"There is not a living thing that is not afraid when it faces danger. The true courage is in facing danger when you are afraid."

- L. Frank Baum, The Wonderful Wizard of Oz

Chapter Five

Resilience
Lessons From So Many

Peter and Tania
The hurricane was unlike anything Peter and Tania had ever been through. The wind sounded like a train, and even in the shelter where they went, they heard the windows breaking, and power was out except for the emergency generators. Everyone was scared. Babies cried, dogs shuffled around the gym floor trying to get to a safe and comfortable place to lie still. At one point when they heard part of the roof get torn off, they thought it was over. Even here it was just not safe.

When the hurricane finally was over, Peter and Tania tried to get back to where their home had been. But when they left the safety of the shelter, they quickly learned that nothing was there. The flooding was extensive, and it looked like a war zone. Whole neighborhoods were just rubble. While shocked, they both knew that they had made it, they had survived! And with time they would bounce back, all the way. Perhaps, in the spot where their house had been, they could find something- a picture, a personal object, that they could take with them as they started on the road back.

We know that between 2 and 25 percent of people who have been through different types of trauma will develop Posttraumatic Stress Disorder (PTSD). That means that most people will not. What do we know about these people? Some have referred to those who survive a trauma, but don't show the signs of PTSD or other psychological problems, as "resilient".

Resilience is defined as "the ability to recover from a shock without permanent after effects". One way to think about resilience is to think about the movie "Unbreakable," where Bruce Willis played David Dunn. David Dunn was an individual who, despite being in a train wreck and having horrible things occur to him, would walk away unscathed, the only survivor.

Resilience in its psychological application actually started as a term attributed to children. Some children, despite growing up in horrible situations, seem to turn out all right. They survive abuse, neglect, poverty, terrible conditions and despite all that, they become strong, capable human beings. This term, resilience, was taken from the child psychological literature. Some children were observed to withstand tremendous hardships, and extremely difficult upbringings, and still looked pretty normal. Other children in similar settings understandably carried these hardships with emotional scars and never really recovered psychologically. The children who did well were termed as "resilient" or showed a "hardiness". This term was borrowed, and then applied to include not just children, but to adults as well, who exhibited this ability to get through tough situations without expected or even predicted psychological difficulties.

There are a number of definitions for resilience including:

- The ability to recover from a shock without permanent after effects.
- The ability to adapt well to unexpected changes and events, and stressful situations.
- Characterized by the ability to bounce back and cope with bad or difficult situations.
- Bend but not break under stress.

- Rebound from adversities.
- To handle setbacks. To persevere & adapt.
- To maintain equilibrium following bad or traumatic events.

Ernest Hemingway stated – *"The world breaks everyone and afterwards many are strong in broken places."*
Friedrich Nietzsche believed – *"That which doesn't kill me makes me stronger."*
Zimmerman & Arunkumar argued – *"Resilience is not a trait that a youth is born with ... it is a complex interactive process."*

So, we've heard a number of different definitions, but it's still unclear what exactly we mean when we say someone is resilient. Is it a temporary state? Is it a time when during the moment of horror, a person shows the qualities that help them overcome the adversity? Is it a trait? A set of enduring, personal qualities that show up over a lifetime? If it is a temporary state, what makes it occur in some and not others? What thoughts, actions or reactions foster it and allow it to occur?

Resilience seems to be related to a number of concepts, some clear, others less clear. In earlier psychological literature, people who survived well were as we said, to show a type of "hardiness", to bear up well in times of trouble; others were described as having a flexibility, which allowed adaptation in times of adversity. If it is a set of "skills" or "attributes", how do you measure it? Better yet, can you teach those skills and attributes? Let's look at those questions.

Measurement of Resilience

As with most measures of psychological concepts, how you think about it determines how you measure it. There is at the time of this writing, no agreed upon best way to measure "resilience". There have been a number of scales constructed, one of which we'll mention here.

The Albany & Memphis Resilience Scale (AMRS) was constructed as part of a study conducted by the University at Albany with Dr. Sharon Danoff-Burg and Memphis University with Dr. Gayle Beck, which looked at how well college students, coped with stressful life events. The scale was designed to measure many of the major components of resilience such as 1) coping, 2) cognitive flexibility, 3) finding meaning in the event, 4) spirituality, 5) belief in one's strength, and 6) how well one recovers from the stress. The AMRS uses a 0-4 scale for the items, with 0= not at all like me or strongly disagree, while 4 = a great deal like me, strongly agree. The scale was designed to measure qualities that have been associated or tied to "resilience". Remember the scores are not used to show who is resilient and who is not, but rather as a way to let you get a sense of the extent to which you may or may not have qualities that have been tied to being resilient.

Here is the scale:

The Albany & Memphis Resilience Scale (AMRS)

Instructions: The following statements describe how you recall dealing with stressful life situations. Please indicate the extent that each statement is true of you. There are no right or wrong answers, only responses that reflect how you rate your reaction. Please use the following rating scale (0=Not at all like me and a 4=Exactly like me), to rate how well you think these statements describe your reaction during and after your most stressful events.

I ...	Rate from 0-4
1. ... am able to cope in a positive way.	_____
2. ... am able to deal with whatever happens.	_____
3. ... am made stronger from dealing with the event.	_____
4. ... use prayer to help cope.	_____
5. ... am able to deal with negative feelings and emotions	_____
6. ... don't feel sorry for myself.	_____
7. ... bend but don't break with the challenges and problems.	_____
8. ... usually take things in stride.	_____
9. ... have gotten through adversity and hard times before.	_____
10. ... can usually see more than one way to solve a problem.	_____
11. ... believe my personal life has meaning.	_____
12. ... tend to stay true to my values in life.	_____
13. ... don't avoid things that make me feel bad.	_____
14. ... find meaning from both good and bad experiences.	_____
15. ... can handle a number of things at the same time.	_____
16. ... always bounce back from hard times.	_____
17. ... don't worry about things longer than I need to.	_____
18. ... think of myself as an optimistic person	_____
19. ... understand that I am not the only one things like this happen to.	_____
20. ... tend to see the spiritual importance of coping with things.	_____
21. ... learn from every situation, even bad ones.	_____
22. ... have learned to take one day at a time.	_____

- Adapted from Hickling, E.J., Beck, G. , and Danoff-Berg, S. (2009).

Now that you've taken the scale, it should be a little more clear why we ask, "What exactly is being measured?" The scale asks not just about how well you bounce back, but also asks about spirituality, how you make sense out of the world, and how comfortable you are with bad feelings. Why? Well, most studies have looked at resilience as either an absence of psychopathology (or bad reactions after a trauma), or have tried to learn from those who did well after trauma, and see how they might be different from those who didn't do so well. They also try to apply our understanding of what kinds of thoughts, feelings and behaviors help one cope. So, a scale has to have a lot of different questions to try to include all those areas. We have not done any studies to show exactly what the scores show, but as a guideline, scores less than 44 would suggest low resilience, 45 – 68 moderate resilience, and scores greater than that to indicate high resilience. Again, it's a self-report measure, and doesn't mean that you are or aren't resilient, but it gives you an idea of how you respond on a scale of this.

Resilience Training

Martin Seligman, a psychologist at the University of Pennsylvania and his team, has developed what they term a Resilience Training Program. They looked at the psychological literature including their own studies, and asked what we can take from our current knowledge to develop preventative programs for use where we know high stress and trauma is likely. One such important situation was with our wars in the Middle East. The Resilience Training Program (RTP) worked with our military troops before they were deployed to these highly stressful situations. They looked at what are believed to be protective factors, or factors that are thought to lead to resilience in the face of stressful or traumatic events, and then designed a program around them. Those protective factors briefly include:

- Optimism
- Effective Problem Solving
- Faith
- Sense of Meaning
- Self-Efficacy
- Flexibility
- Impulse control
- Empathy
- Close relationships
- Spirituality

The resilience training program created educational activities to provide the related skills and information on those topics over several days as an intensive immersion into resilience training. The goal was to try to help make soldiers psychologically stronger so that they can bear up to the horrors and rigors of a war situation. The concepts are beginning to look familiar aren't they? Those things that put one at risk for PTSD, and those things that helped prevent PTSD (like being willing to endure uncomfortable feelings so as to not have to avoid the feelings) are now showing up in the resilience work.

It's good to know that the government is using what psychologists and others have learned about trauma and resilience, but how does that help us learn how we can foster our own resilience? How can we try to strengthen our own qualities to survive better, or try to learn those skills that may give us some relief from the negative impact of trauma?

Fortunately, there are some resources that are readily available to help. The American Psychological Association has provided a list of 10 things that they believe can help promote resilience.

10 Ways to Build Resilience

1) **Make connections.** Good relationships with close family members, friends, or others are important. Accepting help and support from those who care about you and will listen to you strengthens resilience. Some people find that being active in civic groups, faith-based organizations, or other local groups provides social support and can help with reclaiming hope. Assisting others in their time of need can also benefit the helper.
2) **Avoid seeing crises as insurmountable problems.** You can't change the fact that highly stressful events happen, but you can change how you interpret and respond to these events. Try looking beyond the present to how future circumstances may be a little better. Note any subtle ways in which you might already feel somewhat better as you deal with difficult situations.
3) **Accept that change is a part of living.** Certain goals may no longer be attainable as a result of adverse situations. Accepting circumstances that cannot be changed can help you focus on circumstances that you can alter.
4) **Move toward your goals.** Develop some realistic goals. Do something regularly -- even if it seems like a small accomplishment -- that enables you to move toward your goals. Instead of focusing on tasks that seem unachievable, ask yourself, "What's one thing I know I can accomplish today that helps me move in the direction I want to go?"
5) **Take decisive actions.** Act on adverse situations as much as you can. Take decisive actions, rather than

detaching completely from problems and stresses and wishing they would just go away.

6) **Look for opportunities for self-discovery.** People often learn something about themselves and may find that they have grown in some respect as a result of their struggle with loss. Many people who have experienced tragedies and hardship have reported better relationships, greater sense of strength even while feeling vulnerable, increased sense of self-worth, a more developed spirituality, and heightened appreciation for life.
7) **Nurture a positive view of yourself.** Developing confidence in your ability to solve problems and trusting your instincts helps build resilience.
8) **Keep things in perspective.** Even when facing very painful events, try to consider the stressful situation in a broader context and keep a long-term perspective. Avoid blowing the event out of proportion.
9) **Maintain a hopeful outlook.** An optimistic outlook enables you to expect that good things will happen in your life. Try visualizing what you want, rather than worrying about what you fear.
10) **Take care of yourself.** Pay attention to your own needs and feelings. Engage in activities that you enjoy and find relaxing. Exercise regularly. Taking care of yourself helps to keep your mind and body primed to deal with situations that require resilience.

Additional ways of strengthening resilience may be helpful. For example, some people write about their deepest thoughts and feelings related to trauma or other stressful events in their life. Meditation and spiritual practices help some people build connections and restore hope.

The key is to identify ways that are likely to work well for you as part of your own personal strategy for fostering resilience.

APA WEB SITE: http://www.apa.org/helpcenter/road-resilience.aspx

SEE ALSO: http://www.apa.org/helpcenter/resilience-war.pdf

Looking at the previous list, there are a number of important and helpful ideas:

1) One of the main points is how our thinking can greatly affect what happens next. What this means is that the way we think about ourselves and about what has happened to us will be different for different people and will have a very important effect on how the trauma works in our lives. The APA recommends that we don't want to become rigid in our views and see things just one way. We want to make sure that we are adaptable and flexible in terms of how we think about what is occurring to us, and be willing to change or adjust the way we think about ourselves and what has happened.

2) Related to this is the idea to keep things in perspective. When horrible things occur, quite naturally they dominate our lives; they take over. Yet people do survive them. People survive wars, people survive hurricanes, and people survive terrible disasters. People come through them. How one sees the horrible events and the way you manage the events is important. While it's certainly difficult, people do surmount these events. What we are trying to do with this suggestion is to foster the perspective that it's possible to survive well, and it's how we view the traumatic event and ourselves and others that greatly impacts what happens to us next.

3) Another idea is that of seeing the trauma as a time of self-discovery, such as looking for opportunities within the traumatic event and its aftermath for learning more about oneself. This idea speaks to the notion that even within terrible events we perhaps can learn something new or unexpected about ourselves. Or perhaps we discover something reaffirming about ourselves. A key question can be what has this experience taught me? What did I learn about myself that I only learned by having this very tragic experience? These kinds of questions are believed to help people survive, and in fact, to deal well with these tragic and traumatic situations.

4) Maintaining a hopeful outlook is important. People who have hope do better than people who feel hopeless. This can show up in thoughts like, "Things may work out. Things can work out." On average, people who believe that things will work out certainly seem to do better than people who don't. This is an idea that we can all carry in our hearts. Whether we fully believe it or not, the outlook, the way of thinking, and then believing, is important. This is a lesson we learn from those who have done well following life's traumas.

5) Acceptance of change is important. Most of the time we don't want the things that follow a tragedy, such as the losses, the pain. We want things to remain as they were, never having had to suffer the trauma. However, change is an important part of life. Nothing stays the same. Whether a tenant of Buddhist philosophy, or whether just a practical way of looking at the world, we know for certain that nothing is going to remain as it is. Sometimes the changes are positive and sought after. Things like new relationships, better health, and promotions. Life, however, is not just positive changes. Tragic situations, traumatic events, are also part of change. This willingness to see pain as well as joy, is something, whether we like it or not, we need to accept. The better we can have that acceptance, the more resilient we are in dealing with this and moving on in our lives.

6) Since change is an important part of life, engaging in activities that provide conditions for change is a good thing as well. Being around people who are good at change, being in situations that allow us to deal with new things on a regular basis helps us to learn the traits and skills to change well. The idea that we need to stay connected or reconnect with people is also noted as an important path for dealing with a tragedy and for fostering our resilience.

7) Goals are an important part of resilience. If you know what you are trying to do, to get better, to get back to your family, to have some reason for moving as opposed to staying still, it often helps us move in a positive way. Set goals that are both short term and long term. This may be as simple as doing rehabilitation exercises, or lifting 5 more pounds in weights. It may also be to resume your life as fully as you can in as short a period of time as possible. Setting goals seems to help people deal with bad times more effectively and to move towards a more valued life.

8) Decisive actions are also important. Being passive, allowing things to happen, while sometimes necessary, is also contrary to resilience. Making a plan, taking action, doing something, often makes us feel we have more power and in some way can impact the outcome.

9) Make corrections. If things do not work, do not keep doing the same things. Let's try to make corrections in our activities, whether they are internal, ways that we are thinking about ourselves, the way we are dealing with things, or with things that we are doing outside of ourselves. Albert Einstein's definition of what insanity is, "doing the same thing over and over again and expecting a different outcome", certainly applies here.

10) Take care of yourself. When we have had something bad happen to us, what better time to take good care of ourselves. If we have a physical wound, such as a cut, we take care of it. We do this by cleaning the wound, putting medicine on the wound, maybe even getting stitches, dressing the wound and making sure it has a chance to heal. The same should be true for our emotional healing. Very few of us actually do this and the same analogy applies. Do the things that you know can help take care of yourself, both physically, and emotionally.

11) Lastly, stay connected. We are social creatures. We benefit from the contact of others who love and care about us. Doesn't it make sense that when you are in pain, and suffering, that any instinct to pull away will not be a wise move for most people? While we all may have moments where we need to pull away to regroup, the feeling of being connected has been found over and over to be a powerful way to help healing occur.

These 11 things, while not all inclusive, show a path that can help people deal and cope well with tragic, traumatic situations.

What doesn't help?

Now, what do we know that doesn't help resilience? What is it that can actually get in the way?

Here we're going to draw on some of the work of the distinguished psychologist, Donald Meichenbaum. Perhaps as much as anyone, Dr. Meichenbaum has studied and worked with the area of trauma and resiliency. Let's take a very small part of his work, and see how it might further our thinking on resilience and our learning about how to apply resilience to our lives.

One of the main points Dr. Meichenbaum makes is how many people who develop problems after their trauma take on the stance or perspective of a victim. They begin to view themselves as someone who is now much more vulnerable to further injury; they feel defeated, they focus on their failings and imperfections, and they think over and over about how close they came to even worse injury. There may be thoughts like, "What might have happened?" "I'm damaged!" or "I can't shake these memories".

Second, they begin to see the world through a set of beliefs that keep the negative view in place. By this we mean that they see the negative changes as permanent, they believe that the unsafe, unpredictable nature of the world is stronger than ever, and, perhaps most damaging, they believe that life has lost its meaning. Thoughts may include things like, "I don't feel human anymore", "I have no control over anything", or "I will never be happy again." Other thoughts can include thinking negatively about the past, the present or the future. Once again, we are going to be starting to look at how thoughts affect what happens and how we feel. If I am looking back and I am filled with negative ideas about my past, about things that have occurred, it does not seem to help move me in a positive direction or to get through situations as well as other thoughts which do not do these things.

Third, blame becomes a focus along with anger. Thoughts might involve a sense of "deserving" the pain. That they've been "wronged" and that, "Life is unfair, and I need to get even!" The idea that life will never be the same contains only the ongoing pain and suffering. In some sense, if we stay stuck with things that we could have done, should have done, and feel guilty for having done or not done, it perpetuates the problem and makes it hard to move forward.

Blame can include both self blame or blaming others. "If not for them, this would not have happened."

Again, you are starting to see the trend. How we think about things, where we attach significance, blame and energy, can keep us stuck or it can help us deal with adversity in a more positive way. Near misses are sort of like this. They are incidents that remind us that "it almost happened again", whether that someone who cut in front of me could have almost caused another tragic accident, or whether the storm that came up the coast just missed and could have been another horrible, destructive hurricane. Near misses or tragedies we read about in the newspaper or see on the TV often remind us of how precious and dear life is. But rather than lead to joy or appreciation, it is striking for some survivors, how easy it is to see it as keeping us vulnerable and at risk. If this idea stays in our minds, it can cause our perceptions of near misses and near occurrences to keep us stuck in a place of pain and fear.

Even in survival, it becomes common to think about how it could have been even worse. That the world is now a place where one can never feel safe. Much like hypervigilance; we are on guard all the time. You might feel as if you "live in fear because danger is everywhere, and if I am not on guard, I will once again have something horrible occur". It seems like a protective and adaptive way to think after surviving a horrible event, BUT it does not help people move forward.

Meichenbaum illustrates how there are A NUMBER OF THINGS YOU CAN DO TO PERPETUATE PTSD, including the use of drugs and alcohol to avoid feelings; to continually ruminate, to think over and over about the event with no break or distraction. He points out how many people argue that they will act more positively or in a way that is encouraged, "when I begin to feel better". So you may hear things like, "I do that when... (fill in the blank with your thought or reaction) happens," or "I want to do that BUT..

(fill in the blank)...stops me". So again, change does not occur. One stays stuck, and suffering.

Some people keep many of the details of the trauma secret, even from those who are trying to help them such as doctors and therapists. Then, in part these individuals, by holding onto the secret, almost become defined by the secret as something so powerful I can't even tell those who are most open to hearing that secret. It becomes a thought like, "I have this secret problem I'm trying to deal with that I can't tell anyone". Individuals who act in this way are not defined then by all the other aspects of their life- their relationships with others, how they do their job, their values and actions, but by this secret. If they think only about what has been lost, if they cannot get over their injury, their lost wages, their friends, the things that have been changed and forever gone as a result of what has occurred, not only are they stuck back there, but they are no longer living in the present and no longer able to move forward in the way that we saw in the earlier table.

Last there are a number of things that people DON'T DO, which keeps them feeling bad. These include not seeking out friends to help. One area we will revisit over and over is the role that social support (friends and family) can play in helping people get over their trauma. But for many, the pain and suffering makes this a hard path to travel. The same is said of faith and support in our beliefs. Many will say they have lost their faith, that the loss and the trauma, and the senselessness of the pain and suffering, make them question their faith. Others have found their faith to be of great comfort in finding their way after a tragedy.

The use of "contrafactual thinking" according to Meichenbaum feeds this process. What is contrafactual thinking? This describes a way of thinking that doesn't rely on the facts, but relies more on our views that are now distorted, or not as logical or clear as they once were. An example of this would be, "If only I had done that, things would have worked out". "If not for that, it could have been better." These are ways of changing the facts, trying to reconstruct events or memories so it would work out differently; "If only I had driven down a different street, the accident would not have happened." "If only I had been five minutes later, my friend would not have been killed." These kinds of ideas make up new facts that do not help resilience, but in fact, keep us stuck and blaming ourselves in a way that perpetuates the problem.

Dwelling on our negative reactions also can impact us. If I think about how I am going to constantly stay depressed, worried, or have been changed in any negative fashion, it is hard to believe that things can change in a positive way. This seems to impact resilience in a way which stops it from occurring as well.

Comparing oneself with others negatively is another way of coming up short. "Others have done this well. How come I am not able to get through this kind of experience as well as they did?" "I **should** be stronger. There **must** be something wrong with me." These negative self comparisons adversely affect the kind of change that we are hoping for. It becomes easy to think that somehow it's different for others, that "They are feeling better, why is it taking me so long?" "Shoulds" and "musts" in our thinking, and similar absolute rules, need to be noted and examined.

When you avoid certain situations, decide not to go near things that remind you of the event, do things to avoid activities that might make you more social, such actions weaken one's resilience.

And then there is the idea that somehow there must be some meaning in this situation, but I can't seem to find it. Thoughts such as, "Why this person died, and why I survived? I can't seem to understand. It makes no sense to me and I feel more hopeless and displaced than ever".

Resilience is an important topic. How some people seem to weather these storms of trauma and do it so well holds valuable lessons for those of us who are trying to deal with ours. As we are going to see in future chapters, there also seem to be common threads that help with how we deal with the problems, how people have avoided problems and, as we are about to learn, how we can even grow following these traumatic events and tragedies.

Recap

Looking at the big picture on resilience, a central concept is the idea of "changing our personal narratives". What does this mean? This means that, somewhere in our heads, we think about ourselves and about what has happened in certain ways. We have our stories, or narratives. Narratives are the ways we describe what has happened and is happening to us. Most of these narratives include some truth, some mistakes that are usually related to our worst fears, and a lot of perceptions and misperceptions about ourselves, others and the world. We do not want to become fixed in our narratives and see things just one way. We want to make sure that we are adaptable and flexible in terms of how we think about what is occurring to us and that the world adapts and adjusts with the way we think about ourselves and what has happened.

The second idea is to keep things in perspective. Horrible things will, at times, try to dominate our lives; they take over. Yet people do survive them. People survive wars, people survive hurricanes, and people survive terrible disasters. People come through them and this is important for each of us to see. Most people, who are in many ways just like you, survive and go on with their lives. Please find some comfort in that. There has never been anyone exactly like you. Give yourself the same benefit that you might give others that you are doing the best you know how to do in a hard situation. Hopefully by the end of this book, you will have found ways to do it even better.

The third idea, looking for opportunities for self-discovery, speaks to the notion that even within terrible events we learn something about ourselves. What is it this experience has taught me? What did I learn about myself that I only learned by having this very tragic experience? These kinds of questions help people survive, and in fact, deal well with these tragic and traumatic situations.

Maintaining a hopeful outlook is important. People who have hope do better than people who feel hopeless. Things may very well work out. Things can work out. People who believe that certainly do better, and this is an idea that we can all carry in our hearts. Whether we fully believe it or not, the outlook is important.

"I am not afraid of storms, for I am learning how to sail my ship."

- Louisa May Alcott (1832-1888)

Chapter Six

Posttraumatic Growth
Good from Bad?

Carlos's story continued...

Over time, Carlos began to see the world differently than he had originally. At first he was just overwhelmed, with so much pain, anger, and loss. But after a while he began to find some subtle, and important changes that were occurring in him. While a warrior, and someone who had to perform many acts in the line of duty that he would never share fully with others, he saw the importance of his work, and in it the sanctity of life. He saw a renewed faith grow, seemingly out of nowhere. He had thought his soul was barren, but instead he saw with a fierce pride, his ability to care for and protect his family, his wife and their new son. He felt love and saw it as a miracle, not to be taken for granted. He knew he had done things only a strong person could have done; but also realized that even strong people can carry wounds. And that requires strength too. It wasn't that the memories and the nightmares were completely gone. They weren't. He would honor those he'd lost with his decisions about life if he could. This idea helped him see the values in his life he held dear, even as he saw the terror of how he arrived to hold them.

So far we have talked about stress reactions that can follow tragic situations and traumas. We've talked about resilience, how some people seem to weather very bad situations well and others don't. There is a third response that can also happen following life's tragedies. This response is called growth, in particular 'posttraumatic growth".

Friedrich Nietzsche said, "That which does not kill me can only make me stronger." It turns out that this isn't exactly true. Our research, and my own clinical and life experiences suggest instead, "That which doesn't kill me "erodes" me or wears me down over time".

But the idea of something good following trauma has been followed up by two prominent psychologists, Tedeschi and Calhoun, who have coined the term "posttraumatic growth" (PTG) which refers to the positive psychological change that is experienced as a result of this **struggle** with highly challenging life circumstances.

So what exactly is posttraumatic growth?

Posttraumatic growth is comprised of several things.

In particular there are five major areas that are believed to be related to posttraumatic growth. These include 1) being open to new possibilities, 2) a change in your relationships following the trauma, 3) the increased sense of personal strength, 4) a greater appreciation of life in general and 5) a spiritual change and deepening of one's beliefs. Overall, while one finds oneself more vulnerable, having been changed by the traumatic event, in a very unexpected way, people may come out of tragic circumstances to find themselves as stronger and more capable of dealing with the fundamental issues of one's mortality and life's purposes. That is PTG.

Well, that's all very nice but how do we do that? There are several things that seem to be important to promote growth following trauma. A list of factors promoting growth can be found in the following:

Factors believed to contribute to PTG

- Personality, openness to new experience, extraversion, optimism

- Managing distressing emotions
- Support & disclosure
- Cognitive Changes, giving up certain beliefs to move on
- Cognitive Processing rather than Rumination
- Wisdom and Narrative Development
- Ongoing and Interactive process and outcome

First, some personality types, particularly people who are open to new experiences may experience PTG. Typically, those who are more optimistic and outgoing seem to be more open to growth. This makes sense, that even if something is not a good experience, that if one has a tendency to try to be outward in one's approach, talking with other people and being open to taking from whatever life gives, whatever and whenever that is possible, such a person will probably be open to growth. It also is thought that openness tends to be the opposite of avoidance or trying to cover up unwanted negative feelings or memories. Again, some things hold us constant (such as avoidance), and some allow us to change (openness to new things), as all things change, whether we are open to them or not.

Thus, the post trauma experience leaves us more vulnerable in some ways yet stronger in others, and perhaps even better able to access and express the deep values embedded in our lives. These values can find expression especially when things are trying and require soul searching and a change in one's circumstances such as when you have no choice but to deal with the aftermath of trauma, loss or personal injury.

Another capability, which seems to lead to posttraumatic growth, is the ability to manage distressing emotions that can accompany trauma memories. The people who seem to be able to manage those emotions often have a better capability for being open to growth. That is why all those skills, all those lessons learned from how we treat the most serious responses to trauma, PTSD, can be helpful to all of us as we go through these experiences. It's hard, sometimes impossible to stay with and manage all of the overwhelming emotions and thoughts that can follow some traumas. The people who somehow find a way to grow, seem to be better able to weather those storms, and to manage the turbulence of those feelings.

What promotes growth?

Growth is also promoted by being supported by the people around us in the world and being able to disclose what happened to those people in a supportive and positive environment. Again, this makes sense. We are not alone in this life. We need other people. When we have supportive people who look to us with care, with concern and a desire to help us through our most terrible times, such experiences can often be a powerful and helpful force. When you couple this support and comfort with the capability of sharing very personal, very private, very painful experiences and disclosing them in a supportive, positive way, it can be an important ingredient for helping us grow from these painful experiences. Perhaps in the telling of the story of the trauma to someone who cares and wants the very best for us, we are able to find meaning, purpose and growth from our own tragedy. From the time of childhood, most of us have loved stories that told of a character who met adversity and somehow not only survived, but grew from the tragedy to create a better world for themselves and others.

Epictetus: Greek Philosopher 50-120 AD

- *Men are disturbed not by things that happen, but by their opinion of the things that happen.*
- *It is not what happens to you, but how you react that matters.*

- *For it is not death or hardship that is a fearful thing, but the fear of death and hardship.*

Story of the Asian farmer and a Horse

There once was an Asian farmer who found a horse.... his neighbors were all excited for him and exclaimed, "How lucky you are!" "Maybe", was all he said. A few days later the man's son was riding the horse, and he fell off and broke his leg. "How unfortunate for you, now you won't get any help with the crops, and the harvest is almost upon us!" "Maybe", the farmer replied. A few days later, the emperor sent his soldiers to the town to gather up all the eligible young men to be conscripted into the army. The son of the farmer was not taken, due to the broken leg.

Lucky, or not? It's all in how we look at something where our reaction lies.

Cognitive processing is also an important part of post-traumatic growth. Some people are quick to judge and hold ideas about things while others think differently. Some people just seem more able to change their ideas, to understand that life is not exactly how they first thought it was, and then develop a new way of looking at what happened and to move on. After trauma, this flexibility of thinking is important especially because of the tendency to ruminate about what happened. People get caught up in negative thoughts and get stuck going over and over again with the "what ifs" and how things could have been different as opposed to trying to make sense of it. One way of looking at the repetitive thoughts that stick with someone with posttraumatic stress disorder is that their mind is trying to figure out how to solve this problem, how to find a way that they could have made it turn out differently so as to prevent it recurring, or to make sense of it; while the people who seem to be able to process what happened, make some changes in their thinking and move on, seem to do better.

Related to this is the idea of wisdom. Going through life's tragic moments and life's traumas can provide us an experience, which can give us great wisdom and understanding of ourselves and the world around us. There is a price, and that price is paid in the painful feelings and the tragic losses that occur in most of life's tragedies. However, there may be a wisdom and knowledge gained from this. This wisdom can often be found in the changes in how we think about our personal narratives, how we think about ourselves, how we think about the world and how we plan to interact with the world and others. If we see ourselves for having come through something, some adverse terrible period, as stronger, better, wiser, more deeply enriched by what our understanding of what the world is about, that obviously is a very different experience and narrative than those who see themselves as damaged, limited and never able to move on.

This whole process is an ongoing interactive process. It's not just something that happens in a day. It is something that's worked on over and over again and there is never a real end point to the growth.

Then what isn't posttraumatic growth?

Growth does not mean that people don't suffer. In fact, to be open to the pain, to be vulnerable to what happened, is fairly typical for those who experience growth. Distress is very common following life's tragic events. If you didn't experience significant distress, one would put you in that resilient category. There has been some evidence, in fact, to suggest that if one is totally resilient, there isn't the possibility of much growth. It is only through this pain that one is able to make sense of the world in a new and different fashion.

Now, this doesn't imply that traumatic events are good. They're not. Obviously it would be great if we could go through life without ever having been touched by life's tragedies. But most of us, probably all of us, will in some way or another be touched by life's tragedies. It is what we do with the tragedy that becomes important, not that they are good or bad; they just are. They are a necessary and important part of life.

What isn't PTG?

- Growth does not mean people won't suffer, distress is in fact typical
- Growth does not imply that traumatic events are good, they are not
- PTG is not universal

Posttraumatic growth is also not a universal event. Not everyone grows from traumatic events or grows in the same way. For some people, probably even a minority of people, there seems to be this ability to find, through their own suffering, a sense of positive change. It is from those people that we're trying to learn. We hope that no one suffers a major loss or trauma. But, if you do, we hope that from those ashes, growth may come as well as the pain.

Old Proverb

Man needs a coat with two pockets.

In one is the knowledge that all this is created for him.
In the other is the knowledge we are all too soon dust.

PTG allows for both. One theory, in fact, necessitates that growth only comes if there is enough suffering. Resilience does not require change. Suffering in one form or another may be a needed condition for growth.

We, of course, cannot protect ourselves from major trauma or loss. The point of this book and the people who have worked in this area, such as Tedeschi and Calhoun and others who promote this idea, is that while there is going to be traumatic and tragic events, if it is possible that there is growth as well, it would be nice to figure out how to help more of us achieve that kind of end.

I'm confident that my injuries and getting through my own trauma have added to my own personal growth. I had the choice with several of my scars to have them removed, or to carry them. I chose to keep the scars, even the ones that are obvious, those on my throat and my wrist.

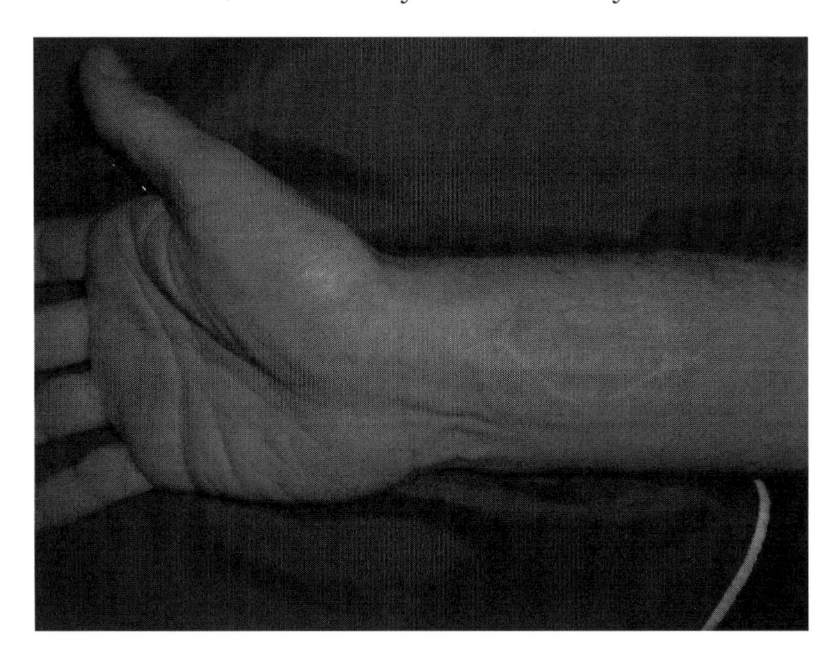

The scars help me remember my experiences and how precious each moment is. They help me remember how hard I fought to get my life back. The hours of pain, the fears, the fortunate successes that came later. They remind me that this life and these experiences are temporary. That life is finite. They remind me of how I chose to deal with each moment as if it were "the most important moment in my life". I believe they also helped me become a better psychologist, to listen better and to respond more fully to those I work with. They definitely helped me appreciate my family and my friendships. Those who were there, who stood by when they were needed are not forgotten. I hope to hold onto the fullness of how much they gave to me. If you asked me if I would be willing to give up these insights not to have gone through the injuries, I would unhesitantly say, "Yes" in an instant. But life's tragedies and traumas aren't ours to take back or alter. They are not choices for us to make. The choice comes in the aftermath, and any positive changes that can come from those events.

True strength does not come out of bravado. Until we are broken, our life will be self-centered, self-reliant; our strength will be our own. So long as you think you are really something in and of yourself, what will you need God for? I don't trust a man who hasn't suffered; I don't let a man get close to me who hasn't faced his wound. Think of the posers you know—are they the kind of man you would call at 2:00 A.M., when life is collapsing around you? Not me. I don't want clichés; I want deep, soulful truth, and that only comes when a man has walked the road I've been talking about.

- Frederick Buechner

6b: The Posttraumatic Growth Inventory

Now that you've read about posttraumatic growth, we'd like to offer you the chance to take a test that can show you on at least one measure how your trauma may have affected you in this area. The scale we're providing is the Posttraumatic Growth Inventory, developed by Richard Tedeschi and Lawrence Calhoun, two of the pioneers in this area. If you find this an area of interest, you are certainly encouraged to go to their website, read any of their books on the topic, or even visit the American Psychological Associations' website and search for the scale. Several references that can serve as a starting point are also included in the reference section in the back of this book.

So how to begin?

First you'll need to take the inventory.

The instructions for taking this scale are straight forward: Read each of the statements and then, based upon a traumatic event that you are thinking about, rate each statement using a 0 (0=I did not experience this change as a result of my traumatic experience) to 5 (5=I experienced this change to a very great degree as a result of my traumatic experience).

Here is the scale:

Post Traumatic Growth Inventory (PTGI)

Please indicate for each of the statements below the degree to which this change occurred in your life as a result of your traumatic experience, using a scale of 0 – 5 where 0= "I did not experience this change as a result of my traumatic experience"; 2= a very small degree; 3=a moderate degree; 4=a great degree, and 5 ="I experienced this change to a very great degree as a result of my **traumatic experience**".

1. My priorities about what is important in life ______
2. An appreciation for the values of my own life ______
3. I developed new interests ______
4. A feeling of self-reliance ______
5. A better understanding of spiritual matters ______
6. Knowing that I can count on people in times of trouble ______
7. I established a new path for my life ______
8. A sense of closeness with others ______
9. A willingness to express my emotions ______
10. Knowing I can handle difficulties ______
11. I'm able to do better things with my life ______
12. Being able to accept the way things work out ______
13. Appreciating each day ______
14. New opportunities are available which wouldn't have been otherwise ______
15. Having compassion for others ______
16. Putting effort into my relationships ______
17. I'm more likely to try to change things which need changing ______
18. I have a stronger religious faith ______
19. I discovered that I am stronger than I thought I was ______
20. I learned a great deal about how wonderful people are ______
21. I accept needing others ______

- Adapted from Tedeschi & Calhoun, (1996)

OK, now that you've taken the test, it's time to score it. There are five scales (or factors) that come from this measure. They are:

1) Relating to others (items 6,8,9,15,16,20, 21)
2) New Possibilities (items 3,7,11,14,17)
3) Personal Strength (items 4,10,12,19)
4) Spiritual Change (items 5,18)
5) Appreciation of Life (items 1,2,13)

Total up each subscale and place the number on the lines below:

Subtotal:
Relating to others ______
New Possibilities ______
Personal Strength ______
Spiritual Change ______
Appreciation of Life ______

The five factors can be compared with other people who have gone through a trauma. The averages don't mean anything more than that, and are provided to simply offer a crude yardstick by which to have you think about what your scores may or may not mean for you.

***Factor I** – Relating to Others: People, who have experienced a trauma on average, score approximately 23 within this category. If you answered with mostly 4's or 5's to a majority of the questions, you may be developing stronger bonds with your loved ones, reestablishing relationships with family or friends you may have lost touch with, and are gaining compassion for others, especially those who may have suffered in ways similar to you.*

Factor II *– New Possibilities: People who have experienced a trauma on average, score approximately 18 within this category. If you answered with mostly 4's or 5's to a majority of the questions, you may be noticing that you are beginning to make choices in a more conscious, aware manner. You are using a plan. You may also be more likely to try to change things that need changing.*

Factor III *– Personal Strength: People, who have experienced a trauma on average, score approximately 15 within this category. If you answered with mostly 4's or 5's to a majority of the questions, you may be expressing greater self-reliance and feeling an improved ability to accept how things turn out. You may be developing a personal strength that can help you through future hardships.*

Factor IV *– Spiritual Change: People, who have experienced a trauma on average, score approximately 5 within this category. If you answered with mostly 4's or 5's to a majority of the questions, you may be reevaluating your spiritual beliefs, are reacquainting yourself with a spiritual community or reconnecting with your own spiritual beliefs.*

Factor V *– Appreciation of Life: People, who have experienced a trauma on average, score approximately 11 within this category. If you answered with mostly 4's or 5's to a majority of the questions, you may be developing a greater appreciation of life as a result of the trauma you went through. This may be experienced as trying to live each day more fully. Other changes may include reprioritizing your personal values and what is important in your life, which may include changes in how you are currently living that life such as spending more time with your family and loved ones.*

If you answered 0 or 1 for many of the items, remember that it can take time to experience change in these areas. As we learned earlier, it can often be the case that only after some time and periods of feeling badly, that growth may come. Posttraumatic growth is an ongoing process that may occur months or years after you experience trauma. You may want to see how you have changed several months or years from now, and take the inventory again.

Prologue to Part II

Transforming Tragedy

In the first portion of this book, we learned about the different reactions that can follow a trauma. There are adverse reactions such as PTSD, where anxieties, depression, and intrusive recollections often negatively affect a person's life. We also spoke briefly about the theories that are believed to answer the question about why PTSD develops, and the types of treatments psychologists use to treat PTSD. We tried to provide information about what is known about trauma and the ways that people react to traumatic events in a way that will be helpful to us as we transform our own personal tragedies.

Second, we learned about resilience. There seem to be a good number of people who get through a trauma without any noticeable or admitted problems. These people have also been studied, and from these studies, different qualities or attributes have been extracted that seem to differentiate this group from those who develop problems.

Last, we introduced the idea of posttraumatic growth. For some people, it seems, there is the possibility of not just surviving a personal tragedy, but to arise from those ashes a changed, and in some ways, a better person. As we explained, it's not that we wish a trauma on anyone; we don't. And I think that almost everyone who has suffered a terrible loss or other bad consequence of trauma would gladly give up whatever growth occurred to not have to bear that tragic moment. Unfortunately, life doesn't give us that choice. If we can learn from those who somehow made positive changes in the aftermath of tragedy, perhaps we can find a way to become the best person possible, and take that along with our pain and regrets on the path of growth into the next chapter of our life.

In Part II of Transforming Tragedy, we will make real the skills and knowledge that can help us begin our own transformations, drawing from the lessons of what is known about the possibilities and the pathways of positive change at this time.

Chapter Seven

Lessons Learned from PTSD, Resilience & PTG

Gloria

Gloria worked as a psychologist in a PTSD treatment center. She'd worked there for 9 years before her trauma occurred. (I will not include the trauma description here as even disguised it might be possible to identify her). She knew all there was at the time to treat PTSD. Yet even with her knowledge and experience she couldn't shake the memories. The images kept haunting her, both during the day and at night when she felt defenseless against them. That was when she came to see me. We talked for quite awhile. What we did was agree to use what we both knew about PTSD, and to spend our time together trying to help as best we could to find a way to help her. We would need more than manuals. We would need more than "clever tricks". It would be a very painful, shared experience back and through all the things she didn't want to carry any longer, but didn't know how to put down and move on. It became all of that, a journey through all of the horrors and memories eventually coming to the other side, with her first accepting and then embracing a way to carry those experiences. It was amazing to see her transform herself into an incredible therapist, and fuller person, rather than someone feeling so destroyed and victimized by what had happened to her.

So what have we learned so far? If we look at all three possible experiences that have been studied following a trauma: 1) adverse reactions including posttraumatic stress disorder and its treatment, 2) resilience, and 3) posttraumatic growth, one lesson stands out above all else - DO NOT AVOID THOSE THINGS THAT ARE CAUSING YOU DISTRESS! It is important to be willing to experience the things that are painful. When we discussed the symptoms of PTSD, one cluster of symptoms included avoidance or efforts to avoid the thoughts, feelings, reminders (including where you go, who you speak with, and your behaviors) of the trauma. When we looked at what puts people at risk for developing PTSD, we found that those who push those unpleasant feelings, thoughts and reminders away did worse. Trying to keep those thoughts and feelings away is not only impossible (remember our elephant experiment!), but it worsens the bad reactions by making the feelings of anxiety stronger each time we temporarily escape from them. The temporary escape only lets us know how much we want to avoid or not feel those things, so we need to focus all of our attention there, and less and less on living our lives the way we want to, or the way we used to.

We learn from our experiences. We carry them with us. So, if we find a way to feel better, even if it's only temporary, we will seek out and repeat that way of finding any relief from the unpleasant feelings that are associated with a traumatic memory. Then, when nothing bad happens when we avoid, we erroneously conclude that the avoidance has worked! An example of learning avoidance as a natural and understandable reaction to trauma would be similar to if we touched a door knob to get out of a room, and we received an electric shock. Learning would instantly take place, we'd hesitate to touch the knob again, and if possible, we'd use another door to leave that room. If we had to touch it, a whole host of feelings might come with our memory, and if possible we'd try to minimize them too. Maybe we'd touch the door quickly to see if there would be a shock, and if not, we'd cautiously proceed. The relief that comes from escaping the feelings is more than enough to keep us from ever willfully grabbing the handle to see if we could endure the feelings that we feared would come. In this way, learning to avoid makes sense. Unfortunately, thoughts, feelings, people, and life are much harder to avoid, especially if we want a full life. This is why decreasing avoidance is such a big deal.

Resilience studies share a similar theme showing that those who did best did not avoid those experiences, emotions or actions that involved memories of the event, or those that limited their future actions. Those people "got back on the horse" quickly. But there was also an ability to "tolerate unpleasant feelings". This is important, because while it's all well and good to say you need to not avoid, it's another to fully face the fact that even in those whom we call resilient, they too are dealing with bad feelings, thoughts and difficult actions. Nearly everyone who endures combat experiences, exposure to death, rape, an assault or horrible accidents and injuries is affected. Resilience does not mean "unfeeling"; rather, how people dealt with the event was the key. There was a willingness and courage to confront those things that were inevitable and a part of life. Other things could be seen as more important than avoidance of pain. This doesn't mean that those who choose to avoid thoughts, feelings or behaviors are weaker or have less courage. That would be wrong, insulting and ignores the fact that we are all different and come from different places. As we're learning more about our own experiences of trauma and it's meaning, we see this is a very personal journey. Each of us will have to find our own way even as we work through this together. No one should sit in judgment of someone else's reactions, or perhaps even our own actions or reactions.

The purpose of this book is to show that ALL REACTIONS are human and occur for a reason, and to learn from those who have dealt with or are dealing with their personal tragedies in ways that can help us realize our own hoped for outcomes.

Last, the lessons from posttraumatic growth support the idea that there will be pain, but out of the pain comes the possibility for growth. We can become more like the people we want to be, we can create the lives we want to live, and we can do what matters to us in our lives. We can appreciate our time here in this life, our unique place, not taking things for granted, appreciating our strengths, and our weaknesses and begin to explore a new perspective that may well take on a spiritual dimension. For some people these changes are held very privately, for others they make very public the new paths they chose to take. They may even describe how the tragedies in their lives have led them in new directions or in ways that can possibly help others who have borne similar pain. We learned in those stories how it is not the avoidance of pain that allows these changes to occur, but rather allowing the pain to come in, be accepted and made a part of who we are in new ways; in ways we never thought possible.

Every experience includes exposure to the things that are painful. There is a beautiful book by a Buddhist master, Pema Chodron, entitled "The Places That Scare Us". The book teaches us that sooner or later, we all will need to confront our demons. The things that have been tragic, the things that are painful, the things that hurt us, and that contribute to our suffering have to be confronted if they are to be carried with less pain. The key seems to be how to do that in a positive fashion. Exposure to painful memories when done correctly can be a good thing, a healing thing. When exposure is done incorrectly, in a way that fails to honor the possibilities that are a part of the pain, it can lead to a strengthening of the drive to avoid and escape painful feelings and memories.

Exposure

There are many types and possible targets of exposure. Remember, what we are confronting can be thoughts, feelings, places, people, or memories. Anything that leads to a desire or an action to **avoid** should be considered as a potential target for exposure. Remember, the purpose of exposure is to reduce the anxiety that comes up when we see things, do things, or think about things related to our traumatic experiences. Ultimately, if we can stop having to avoid things that cause anxiety, our lives can include the flexibility to do what is important to us rather than being controlled by the need to avoid everything that causes pain.

In vivo Exposure (or "in life" exposure): As we learned in the earlier sections, avoidance is often accomplished by staying as far away from those situations that are reminders of our trauma and the uncomfortable feelings and memories they provoke. In vivo (i.e., *actually physically present situations*) exposure involves the systematic presentation of those scary cues or situations, intentionally trying to get those very reactions you are trying to avoid because of the feelings or memories they'll bring up. For example, if you have had a trauma while at war, one might try to get you back on the frontline as soon as possible in order to have you confront those situations that are very similar to the ones where your trauma occurred. If a car crash were the trauma, you would be asked to do things in a car that provoked memories and feelings related to your crash. You would be asked to sit in the car, to go for short rides, until eventually you are asked to go back to the scene of the accident. Obviously, some scenes are easier to do in real life than others. For example, car crashes are easier to simulate as a number of scenes that would bring about the desired reactions, than are other traumas such as rape or combat. But even those scenes might involve being around members of the opposite sex, or around people who are of the same ethnic background as those in the war. Remember, even when using in vivo exposure, the things that we are trying to face, are inside of us. What we are really facing are things that remind us of the scary event, our thoughts, feelings and memories, NOT the actual trauma. The world inside of us is the home to those fears and the source of our suffering. We are exposing ourselves not to dangerous things, but scary things that we hold in our minds.

One of the earliest recorded descriptions of exposure based treatment came not from a psychologist, but from the German writer and scientist, Johann Wolfgang van Goethe and how he dealt with his fear of heights. Goethe described how upon arriving in Strasburg in 1770 he saw a cathedral that was so large, it made a "unique" impression upon him, as well as a way to overcome his fear of heights. To address his fear of heights he climbed to the highest part of the tower, and sat for quite awhile, until he dared to stick his head out, and then later he dared to stand on a platform. He stayed long enough, and went often enough, until one day he noticed he had become "indifferent" to the impression the fears and torments had caused. He went on to describe how he was then able to go on ledges and exposed beams where one needed to go, if one wanted to see significant art or architecture. He also described how it also helped him with mountain trips and geological studies where he needed to be to conduct his studies. So, as one can see, exposure has been around for quite awhile, even before psychologists thought to apply it to modern problems and disorders.

Exposure requires several very important elements. First, the scene must be able to provoke the feelings or reactions you are avoiding. The scene may be similar to the one that reminds you of the trauma, and thereby bring about the reaction (anxiety, fear, etc.), or it may be something new that is avoided such as crowds or places that have become uncomfortable. Second, once the exposure begins, you don't leave the scene or the exposure until the uncomfortable feelings diminish. The theory (and practice) is based on the idea that if you stay with a stimulus (that thing that in real life is provoking the reaction) long enough, your reaction will begin to decrease. Why would that be? Well, first, you HABITUATE or DESENSITIZE to the stimulus over time. One cannot keep up the heightened alarm reaction forever. And as it starts to go down, your association with that stimulus weakens, becoming less and less strong. Second, if you are in a safe place, not a combat scene or one where anyone would actually assault you, and the feelings come, and the memories come but you remain, you are having a new experience. One that is free of a negative consequence. Rattled but still standing, new learning is also taking place. You're learning about how to manage those feelings, gaining in capability and strength as you face that feared situation, and your confidence and ability to manage grows more and more.

One concern however, is that if the commitment to stay in the situation long enough is not there, and you give into the fear or anxiety and stop before the feelings can have the chance to get smaller, it will have the opposite effect as we've talked about in different sections, and can actually increase the anxiety and strengthen the association with the stimulus and the associated feelings or memories. This concern is true of all types of exposure. But now that you know this, you can make sure that doesn't happen, no matter what feelings follow. It is critical that once exposure begins there is sufficient time to allow for the change to follow. This can't be rushed, nor predicted. So plan for more time than you think needed if you are to going to try this. You may want to do this with a mental health professional, although many people have done quite well when they did this themselves.

Imaginal Exposure: Imaginal exposure is often used for a number a reasons instead of or in addition to In Vivo exposure. Imaginal exposure is just what it sounds like, the therapist has the person confronting their trauma memories "THINK ABOUT THEM" instead of actually going out in real life and facing them. Instead of getting back up on the horse, the analogy would be to "Think about getting back up" on the horse. Or, more to real life, think about the car crash you were in, or the assault, or those aspects of the trauma that bring about the adverse reactions. Because remember, trauma is not just what literally happened, it is the narrative, or way we remember it, and carry it around with us. Our mind has been compared to a camera, recording snap shots of feelings, images, and thoughts as the trauma was occurring. But the mind can become all confused, and the images and memories hard to organize. Some aspects of trauma we would never want someone to attempt to recreate. It's one thing to drive a car after a horrible crash, it's another to face the car spinning out of control and smashing into something at high speed. These types of memories, or feelings can better be addressed by recreating the image/memories in an office, and then systematically confronting them long enough, and with enough time and coping skills to actually "master" the reactions that will follow. Again, we're not running away from that which provokes us, but with full knowledge, walking toward it, resolute in our desire to confront the memories and feelings that seem so much in control of our lives that we try to avoid or suppress them.

Looking at this from a psychological point of view, imaginal exposure is where we, in our imaginations (thoughts), imagine the scene. We try to create all of the feelings, the ideas associated with the scene, and the memories over and over again in a way that is safe. This needs to be done in a fashion which is agreeable to most people, so that they willingly face those fears and experiences, more painful than not. It is also usually done with a person trained to be a guide at these difficult times, and someone committed to the journey of getting you through the experiences safely. When these conditions are met, the therapy setting can be an amazingly powerful place.

Graded Exposure: Graded, or graduated exposure simply describes the way the provocative stimuli are delivered. It is rarely the case that it is best to confront the scariest part of one's trauma first. This is the part that has the strongest hold on us, the part that we are most defended against. Instead, most post trauma reactions cover the whole range of things that will provoke us, and a wide range of how strong the reactions are likely to be. Looking at a picture of someone in a uniform is most often less powerful than video images of actual combat, which is often less powerful than actual smells and reenactments (such as used in virtual reality exposure, where one puts on visors and headphones while scents are released in an effort to bring back memories of a traumatic event such as combat). Sitting in a car following an accident is less provocative than being in a car in bumper-to-bumper traffic on a 6-lane highway at 75 mph. The whole idea then is to start simple, using a rating scale which lets us know how upsetting each situation or image is, and then constructing a hierarchy, or ladder of easiest to hardest stimuli/events that relate to the trauma. The scale is called the SUDS scale or SUBJECTIVE UNITS OF DISCOMFORT SCALE (SUDS). The scale ranges from 0 (no reaction) to 100 (worst imaginable reaction). Notice we are not calling it "anxiety" or something that we would argue over what it means, and instead are focusing on the strength of the reaction. This allows one to progress, as one feels capable, up the hierarchy, until one's worst fear is faced and mastered.

An example of a sample hierarchy and SUDS rating can be found in the table below:

SUDS Rating	Stimuli/Event
10	1. Imagine sitting in your car
20-30	2. Sit in your car in your driveway
40	3. Drive around your block on a Sunday morning
45-50	4. Drive to local store in light traffic
60	5. Drive in city with moderate traffic
70	6. Drive on highway in light traffic, off hours
90	7. Drive in highway during rush hour traffic
100	8. Drive to scene of accident and sit there until feeling passes

This is where we take things in a stepwise fashion beginning with the easiest one. Maybe just think about cars if you've been in a car accident, just think about being back in a situation where there was the tragedy, and then stay there long enough until finally the feelings can habituate or get smaller. Then you move up the hierarchy ladder to the next most provocative scene and so on until finally you face the most feared things of all.

One of the important things about using a graded hierarchy, and a SUDS rating, is that you make sure there is a range of events/thoughts that can be rated. You wouldn't want everything to be on the high end, or too difficult at first to even try. Nor would you want it to be all smaller items, with a big jump to the worst one possible. There wouldn't be any learning. You instead look for a good number of possible events, with a range of reactions, knowing that each one takes as long as it takes to master, and you NEVER move ahead until each event has been accomplished and done with minimal reaction. These events can be both invivo, or imaginal, or a mixture of both types of exposure.

Flooding: Another method of exposure starts at the worst memory, and again keeps the individual in that scene as long as it takes until the feelings grow less and less. Imagine if you would that you were scared of elevators, but were forced into one, which was then intentionally stopped between floors. At first the terror would be overwhelming. But, as you are now confronting your worst fear, instead of where it is more easily approached, following this models logical conclusion, at some point the person in the elevator would tire and their reactions would become less and less. While used in some instances, especially for simple phobias like the elevator example, this method is rarely used today for treatments of more complex disorders like PTSD, given the distress it creates in the person (and the therapist as well), particularly as the other methods have been found to be so effective. I recommend that if used, this approach only be tried after consultation and in treatment with a trained, experienced professional.

Exposure can be done as the major part of treatment (in the Reference section look for books on prolonged exposure for greater details) or as part of treatment (in the Reference section look for work that uses Cognitive Processing Therapy, Prolonged Exposure or Stress Inoculation Therapy). Other treatments, such as Eye Movement Desensitization (EMDR), Stress Inoculation Training (SIT), or some of the newer CBT treatments such as Acceptance and Commitment Therapy (ACT), also incorporate some type of exposure in their methods.

However, the take home point, as we look at what seems to be one of the most frequently cited lessons learned in this area, is the idea that we need to go to the places that we most want to avoid if we are to get better. How we do that seems to have a lot of variability, with some using this as the major thrust of treatment, and others letting the individual use therapy or life as a more gradual way to confront those feelings and memories that have stood in the way of where one wants to be with one's life.

Treatments can often use a variety of approaches. Some typically incorporate other skills, which will be brought up in the next few chapters. In psychological treatment, one tries to prepare people for these provocative, exposure-based situations. People are taught ways of talking to themselves, ways of calming themselves down and practicing in the sessions what they might expect so it's not as bad as they might have imagined before they had those tools.

In my own example, and one I've not even told my wife, I had to face my own fear about falling and suffering a fatal injury. But how to best do that? First, I used imaginal exposure. I thought about the fall, hitting the ground, having the pain return, and even in this instance, dying. Not easy things to do. But after a while, I was able to let the thoughts be thoughts, without them being more. They didn't really happen; but I saw them as ideas of my mind. Ideas that provoked reactions, ones tied to memories, but also ones that were trying to keep me safe. I didn't run from the anxiety it produced, but instead welcomed it in. Then, it was time for in vivo exposure. I waited for just the right day, a warm spring day. Totally dry, no rain or moisture for days. I waited until there was no one home. My wife and family had already been upset enough having to be there at the time of my fall, and to see me taken by ambulance to the trauma center. So when they were gone for what I knew would be a good long while, several hours, I did what I had to do, I went out on the roof. And sat. And waited. And I had all the feelings that came, the anxiety, the fear, and the dizziness. And then the lifting of the feelings came along with the knowledge that I would not be beaten by a roof, or by the ideas that my head could create. I may never climb around on a roof doing jobs I used to do in the past, but I knew I could, if I had to. I may never like or enjoy heights as I once did, but I knew at least for this height, for this roof, it was possible to return.

Remember Mary and her Car Crash?

Mary used the hierarchy you saw earlier in this chapter. That was part of her treatment. She did those very acts - sitting in her car, and waiting until the feelings left. She got up early on a Sunday and drove around her block. Again and again she drove, not caring if the neighbors thought she was crazy, but drove around the block because she knew it would take her where she wanted to go. She wanted to be free of the anxiety and fear that had stopped her from living the life she wanted. She kept going through that hierarchy until she finally went to the scene of her accident. At the scene of the accident she first drove the route on which she had the accident and then found a place to pull over. In that spot, where she could see cars coming and going, she remembered her accident. She also saw it was an accident that occurred in the past, and one she carried with her in her memories. On that day, even as she saw a few pieces of her broken tail light on the side of the road, the road became just a road again. The intersection became an intersection that was where she had her accident, but it was no longer any more dangerous than any other place. The longer she sat, the smaller the feelings of anxiety and dread became. In her tears, she expressed how she felt clean, and free. She would never forget the accident, but she could live today without it necessarily getting between her and where she wanted to go.

The idea of change has been planted. ("Though I do not believe a plant will spring up where no seed has been, I have great faith in a seed. Convince me you have a seed there, and I am prepared to expect wonders.")

- Thoreau

Chapter Eight

Cognitive Reappraisal
Thoughts that Hurt, Thoughts that Help

Once there was a young warrior. Her teacher told her that she had to do battle with fear. She didn't want to do that. It seemed too aggressive; it was scary; it seemed unfriendly. But the teacher said she had to do it and gave her instructions for the battle. The day arrived. The student warrior stood on one side, and fear stood on the other. The warrior was feeling very small, and fear was looking big and wrathful. They both had their weapons. The young warrior roused herself and went toward fear, prostrated three times, and asked, "May I have permission to go into battle with you?" Fear said, "Thank you for showing me so much respect that you ask permission." Then the young warrior said, "How can I defeat you?" Fear replied, "My weapons are that I talk fast, and then I get very close to your face. Then you get completely unnerved, and you do whatever I say. If you don't do what I tell you, I have no power. You can listen to me, and you can have respect for me. You can even be convinced by me. But, if you don't do what I say, I have no power." In that way, the student warrior learned how to defeat fear.

- Pema Chodron

Every trauma requires us to think about the trauma, to think about the tragic events. Cognitive reappraisal (sometimes called cognitive restructuring) in some form or another must happen if we are to move past these events. This can be done in many ways. One, as you've already heard, is being exposed to the things we don't want to face. This avoidance applies not just to people and places, but also to our thoughts and feelings. Avoidance of places and people, while at times extremely difficult and painful (such as trying to avoid or not talk with your spouse), is frequently possible. Avoidance of one's thoughts, however, is nearly impossible. This type of avoidance can be attempted by heavy use of drugs, alcohol, extreme forms of distraction, extreme moods (such as anger at an unrelated source), but the thoughts and feelings keep coming back. They have to. They exist inside of you and therefore can't be avoided forever. What's worse, since they are a part of you (and of your mind as it does all this thinking and dealing with the thoughts), they know your every move and are just waiting for the right moment to pop up.

And as we know all too well, just the thought of what happened is enough to cause pain. Why should that be? In part, that's because the thought is tied, associated with the trauma so strongly that it takes on the feeling that we're there, linked psychologically in extremely powerful and clever ways. Some studies have shown we have tens of thousands of thoughts in a day. Most of those we're not even aware of. However, the ones that provoke very strong reactions, such as depression, anxiety, and fear, those are the thoughts we do tend to remember, and those are the types of thoughts we want to avoid and we try to suppress. Suppression, as you've learned earlier, doesn't work very well. Try to keep a thought out of your head.

An analogy of how hard it is to keep a thought at bay is the example of a ball in the water. The ball wants to float, to be on the surface. But if we want to keep the ball off the surface, we need to hold it under water, by use of force. So we hold the ball down. The further down we try to hold it, the more force it requires. We can do it, but after awhile we might get tired or want to do something else with that hand. So then what happens? Up pops the ball. That force is comparable to our psychic force. We can try to hold internal things at bay for a while. But, no matter how strong, or how good we are at holding things down, the very nature of these strong thoughts and feelings will bring them back to the surface. Back into our awareness. And then what are we supposed to do? Keep holding them down, over and over? How well does that work if your aim is to have a full and happy life? All your energy is contained in dealing with those things you didn't really want to deal with, and wish would just go away.

One of the oldest, most central parts of cognitive therapy is to not ignore the thoughts that come up, but to address them head on. To challenge them, and to try to see where they might be wrong, and how those wrong interpretations are causing us to limit our lives and to suffer. Frequently, people who have had a trauma start to see the world as much more dangerous than they did before the trauma occurred. They also tend to see themselves as less capable, more vulnerable, or in some way damaged or weaker. Just take a moment to think how any of those thoughts, if we believed them about ourselves or the world we live in, would make us feel and how they would make us act.

Just close your eyes and think of the event you experienced. Think about how it would be as you imagine yourself back there right now. You can do this as if you were watching it on TV, or in a movie to give yourself some space, but as you do that, just try to quietly sit and observe what changes or shows up in you. What are the images? The feelings? The thoughts that come into your mind? Don't rush away, take a few moments as you allow this to occur. Then gently return to the page.

Now you see the power of thoughts. And as we showed in the earlier chapters, the people who move past traumas well don't fall into these thinking traps, but instead take the thoughts and either dismiss them more effectively, or reinterpret them as more positive, balanced ones that allow them to move forward. A lot of what we are doing in these chapters is helping you find things that will work, and not stay stuck doing the same dysfunctional or painful things over and over again.

"Scars show us where we have been, not where we are going"

- Unknown

Cognitive Behavior Therapy (CBT) 101

Welcome to CBT 101- Cognitive Therapy: Here we are presenting some basic, effective techniques that have been shown to be effective in helping people deal with the after effects of traumatic events. Interested readers can find a selection of books in the appendix if they'd like to learn more about cognitive therapy or to find self-help books specific to cognitive therapy.

Stress Inoculation Training

As previously noted, one of the premier psychologists, who has done considerable work in the area of trauma and how to deal with the psychological aftermath, is Donald Meichenbaum. Several decades ago, he developed a way to help people change their "self talk" that would help them as they faced situations that were likely to produce an unpleasant reaction (such as anxiety or fear). To deal with these situations, coping statements were introduced, with the intent to help begin an "internal dialogue" that will help one manage potentially provocative, disturbing situations. They are called "coping self-statements" as they are produced by the "self", or quite simply, by "You".

There are **three** settings that naturally lead to the use of the coping self-statements.

1. **Preparing for a Stressful Situation:** In life there are a number of situations we can pretty well predict will cause anxiety and stress. These can include places where you will need to confront your memories of the trauma (like at a lawyer's deposition, or when you revisit the place where it occurred, or a place that reminds you of it). Some situations may not even be related to the trauma, but are frankly just stressful places (such as a doctor's visit for a test that you're not sure how it will turn out), and they lead to you being anxious or worried.
2. **Without warning, finding yourself in a stressful situation:** Perhaps you were just going about your day, things seemed fine, and then without warning, you need to confront a stressful situation you hadn't prepared for as you didn't think it could even occur. Examples such as seeing a gang of young men in dark clothes walking toward you and the fears and memories of your rape come over you; or you're driving and suddenly see yourself surrounded by trucks, 18 wheelers, and you have no place to get around them. It had been fine, and now things just changed without warning. How can you cope in these situations?
3. **Dealing with the aftermath of a stressful situation or event:** Coping self-statements can also be applied once a situation has passed. We are judgmental beings. How you think about the situation, and what you did or didn't do, will be impacted, for better or worse by what you're thinking.

So, how does this work? In the table below are a number of coping statements that apply to the three situations (before, during and after) where coping statements can be used. The trick is to first be willing to pause long enough to listen to "what you are already thinking", and then try to substitute in the new coping statements that apply. At first this might seem very artificial. You might even have thoughts like, "This can't work", or "These aren't my real thoughts". If so, you're already paying attention to your thinking, and whether you like it or not, are being influenced by what your mind is telling you. Congratulations, you're on your way.

In this instance we start from that place, and then have you insert thoughts you can control, the coping self-statements. The more you use these types of statements, the more natural they become, and the more likely they will give you the results you are looking for. If you think back to the earlier chapters, you will also recall how it is that this very style of thinking, and the flexibility to not get stuck with uncomfortable, painful thoughts, is what helps explain why some people do better following traumas than other people. Let's have a look.

Positive Coping Self-Statements

The following statements are presented to provide examples of some of the things you can say to yourself in place of the "automatic" thoughts that are negative, and currently occur in stressful situations. If you would like to add some statements that are more in your own words, or more applicable to your unique situation, there is space provided for that purpose. Please feel free to carry this sheet around for your use, until such time as the coping self-statements become more familiar and become a skill you feel you've mastered. Feel free to try different statements in a variety of situations until you find the ones that work best for you.

1. In preparation for a situation that you believe or predict will occur, try the following:
   a) What specific thing do I have to do at that situation or event?
   b) Is there a plan I can develop with steps I can use to deal with this?
   c) This isn't impossible. I can handle it.
   d) No need to worry. Worrying isn't going to help me anyway.
   e) I have a lot of resources. Let's put them to use here.
   f) What is it I'm so scared of?
   g) I have a lot of people who support me. People who deal with this type of problem all the time.
   h)______________________________
   i)______________________________
   j)______________________________

2. During a stressful situation, try to use the following (for confrontation & coping):
   a) I can manage this. I just need to do one step at a time.
   b) I've gotten through tougher things than this before. I won't be overwhelmed. It just feels like that at times.
   c) This situation can be seen as a challenge or an opportunity to get better. It is only a burden or pain if I make it that.
   d) There are very specific things I need to do to get through this (list them out to yourself).
   e) Calm down. Breath. Relax. Slow deep breaths. I got this.
   f) Focus on the present. What do I need to do right now?

g) These feelings are a signal. A signal to use my coping skills. I can expect the fear and anxiety to increase, but those feelings will pass. I can do this.
h)____
i)____
j)____

3. After the situation or stressful event has passed, try the following:
   a) Pay attention to what worked, start there.
   b) Give myself credit for making a good effort, and for any improvement, big or small.
   c) If you consider everything, I did a good job.
   d) I'm learning how to do this. I'll get even better with practice.
   e) I knew I could do this. It just takes some time, practice and effort.
   f) That wasn't as bad as I thought it would be.
   g) I'm making progress. I'm moving in the right direction.
   h)____
   i)____
   j)____

The use of coping self-statements is a skill. It builds on your being able to listen to the automatic negative thoughts (e.g. "this is terrible, I'm going to get hurt", "I can't do this") and allows you the chance to insert statements that do not lead to the same negative feelings. With some success and effort, they can become a natural part of how you respond to the world. They also give you a new skill for understanding what drives some of the adverse reactions like fear and anxiety, and a very concrete thing you can do to try to change what has been occurring inside of you. The techniques are often used in tandem with in vivo exposure or behavioral "experiments" which provide you with evidence to challenge and change some of your thoughts.

How are we going to spend this brief lifetime? Are we going to strengthen our well-perfected ability to struggle against uncertainty, or are we going to train letting go? Are we going to hold on stubbornly to "I'm like this and you're like that?" Or are we going to move beyond our narrow mind? Could we start to train as a warrior, aspiring to reconnect with the natural flexibility of our being and to help others do the same? If we start to move in this direction, limitless possibilities will start to open up.

- Pema Chodron, "The Places That Scare You"

Now, let's build on this skill set to one a little more advanced.

Albert Ellis (among others) and the A-B-C-D Approach

Once you have some appreciation for how to use the coping self-statements, you are ready to learn more about how thoughts can affect how you feel and act. Remember the quote from Epictetus in Chapter 6, where *"It is not the events that shape men's lives, but how we think about them that affects us".* That old Greek philosopher shows very clearly how long human beings have been aware of the power of our thinking and how we struggle to control and lessen the impact negative thinking can have on us. For a related disorder, depression, there are a number of excellent books that address how this can be applied, and interested readers again are urged to look within the appendix for those references.

It is very common for one's view of oneself, the world and **the trauma** to be gravely changed following trauma's aftermath. It's not that we weren't aware that bad things can and will happen to people in life. We see traumatic events all the time in the newspaper, on TV or in movies that we watch. But when it happens to us, we KNOW IT DIFFERENTLY. Now it cuts into our self-protective shell and lets us know it isn't just other people, but any of us that these things can happen to. We are vulnerable, and our illusions of how life is supposed to be get shattered, and challenged.

Part of these shattered assumptions about ourselves and life is that without even being aware, our thoughts can grow very dark, very negative. Perhaps this is why people with earlier traumas and psychological problems hold a somewhat greater risk for PTSD, in that they have inside of them a historical pattern that more easily leads to this way of thinking; It has been speculated that for those people without this history, they have different patterns of thinking that makes it take a little longer to get there. But as we've said, no one is immune to the impact of trauma. This shift in the perception of life being more dangerous doesn't mean the thoughts are accurate, but it does mean if you think in certain ways, you'll feel and act in ways that follow those thoughts. If the world is dangerous, I should feel anxious and I better protect myself, and perhaps avoid even venturing out into it. These feelings and actions suddenly make a lot of sense as they are tied to the thoughts that accompany them.

Now, let's build from the information on the previous page and the work of Albert Ellis, a pioneer of cognitive therapy, who over 50 years ago, began a type of therapy he called Rational Emotive Therapy (RET). He argued that the thoughts were the stuff of therapy, and how to address and change those "irrational" or distorted ways of thinking became a central part of his psychological treatments. He understood that people were not necessarily rational beings, but we were capable of applying logic and argument to problems in thinking, and effecting change in how we feel and act as a result.

This type of cognitive therapy is a direct, easily learned method to understand how our thinking impacts our lives, including our feelings and actions. He used an A-B-C-D model to depict the sequence of events that are occurring in our thinking, and to show how to change the negative interpretations or views that are causing those reactions. One begins by looking at the **A**, the activating event (or antecedent if you prefer). Basically, this is the event; what was it that happened? **B** stands for one's belief, the ideas or interpretations of the situation or appraisal of self, the world or the future. **C** stands for the consequence. The consequence is what you felt or how you acted in the situation. **D** stands for how you can dispute or reevaluate your "automatic" or "irrational" thoughts by substituting more rational or accurate perceptions or beliefs, or at least ones that don't need to lead to such negative outcomes.

So, here is the model:

A = Activating event (What happened?)

B = Belief (What were your thoughts, your perceptions when the event happened?)

C = Consequence (How did you react? What were your feelings? What did you do?)

D = Dispute (Where is the evidence for your B? How can you challenge the belief?)

Let's apply it to this example:

Mary has had a number of panic attacks. Now she is worried that if she is driving on the highway, she would have a panic attack, and possibly kill someone else, or herself. To drive on the highway with this likelihood is "irresponsible", and so she decides not to drive on highways, and only use side roads to get to places she needs to get to. Identify the A-B-C's and Dispute:

A = Panic attacks, and worry of future panic attacks.
B = "It's too dangerous." "To drive is irresponsible, and I could kill someone, including myself"
C = Worry, anxiety, fear. Avoidance of driving on highways.
D = Even if you panic, how do you know you'll have a crash? If you had a crash, how do you know you'd kill someone, or harm yourself? Where is the proof? How well do you see the future? You could have panic on side roads and have an accident as well. You are magnifying the risk, predicting the future and creating a catastrophic event in your head. Nothing has really happened except you are imagining all those events.

(Remember, this is just an example. It takes some time to really get good at this, and one should seek out those references or professionals to help if after reading this, you decide you'd like to learn more than we will cover here.)

We often attribute our feelings, such as anxiety, to external events. I turned off the TV because, "The news made me anxious". Or even positive events such as "I was happy because it was my birthday". But it doesn't take a lot of reflection to realize that birthdays don't make us happy, nor even the people and the presents. We feel happy because we like these people, and they are our friends, and we see this as a good experience to have. Negative reactions are the same as well. Two people, both with similar traumas can watch the same news on TV and one gets upset, and the other doesn't. Why? The answer is in the beliefs held by the two people. One might view the news as a reminder of one's trauma, and how the feelings that are associated are "Too much to bear," or show how they are "Damaged" and "Will never get better". The other person may view the same news with different perceptions, remembering the traumatic experience, but having thoughts that, "I came through a hard time", "I was lucky to get out", "I'm fortunate", "I'm scarred but not damaged in a way that stops me from going after my life, even if I have the scar of the trauma". Thoughts, not the external events, impact our feelings and actions.

So, how does one change a negative appraisal? First you need to see it for what it is, a thought. Let's take the thought, "I'll never get over this". To dispute a thought like that we begin with the first disputing question, "Where is the evidence for that belief?" Just because you've gone this long, doesn't mean it will be forever. "How good are you at predicting a future event?" As we learned in earlier chapters, some thoughts surround how things would be different if others or the world had only "operated by our rules". "That teenage driver shouldn't have run the red light!" There is no argument it would have been better, and one would have preferred that that person hadn't run the red light causing the accident; but people make mistakes all the time. It is human nature to make mistakes. We are not perfect. So, how does the belief that "He shouldn't ...." hold up to the evidence? One last example is provided that tries to get to the self recriminations about how things would have been different, if only..."If only, I left 5 minutes later", "If only, I did X instead of Y". Again I simply ask, how do you know it would have been better? It might have been better, or it might have even been worse! You just made up a story that says I would have avoided the trauma if I did something different. Often at that time I ask, "How do you know it wouldn't have been worse? That instead of X, Z would have occurred, and you would be dead!". The approach is not about winning the argument, but rather illustrating how it is our thinking that leads to negative feelings and limits how we are able to live our lives, and then developing more adaptive views to lead the life we'd like. I try never to underestimate the power of our thinking.

There are some common "distortions" that can occur in our thinking following a trauma. These include:

- *Over prediction of your future fear when confronted with something that will remind you of the event*
- *Over prediction of your future danger when in a threatening situation*
- *Heightened attention to potential threats in the world around you*
- *Decreased appreciation of your own safety when in the environment*
- *Minimizing your own skills and attributes*
- *Minimizing the skills and intentions of others*
- *Catastrophizing the outcome if a future adverse event were to occur*
- *Minimizing your own ability to cope and deal with future negative events, which of course are an inevitable part of life*

Thoughts are very powerful. As you've seen in this illustration, one approach to dealing with our thoughts is to argue with them, challenging them by using our logic and ability to shift perceptions. The main idea here is if a compelling argument is made against where our misperceptions lie, we can change our thinking and thereby change the way we feel. If somehow in the dialogue either between two people, or you and your own mind, a belief is engendered that can help you *see and believe the alternative view,* even though not your first thought, change can happen. These new thoughts, as they fit a "truer, verifiable reality", can often hold greater credence and accuracy than the ones we've held onto in our distorted, inaccurate views of the world and our selves since the trauma. This cognitive approach to treatment of psychological problems, has the greatest research support in our treatment literature. It is, however, not perfect, and should in my opinion be viewed as an important step along the way as we continue to learn more about what it is that can help people through the period after they experience their trauma. It's good. But we need to get better.

Two Monks and a Lady

Two monks were walking down a muddy road in meditative silence, when they came upon and elegantly dressed woman trying to cross the road, without pausing, one monk picked up the woman and carried her to the other side, and then resumed walking. Several hours went by until finally the younger monk said, "I'm sorry to speak so, but why did you pick up that woman? I didn't think monks were supposed to act like that." The older monk turned to the other and said, "I put that woman down hours ago, why are you still carrying her?

- Anonymous

Isn't that something we would all like to do at some point? Yet how do we do that? Sometimes we can problem solve, sometimes we can rationalize an answer, and other times we must just allow the thoughts to be thoughts, and try to carry them gently as we move forward in our lives.

Perhaps the power of our thinking is expressed in the following:

There is an old Buddhist view of the world that people are, "*caught up in regrets from the past and worries of the future.*"

During my trauma, its aftermath, and in my rehabilitation, I certainly experienced many worries, anxieties and fears about what was occurring, what might happen next, and how it was I arrived at such a spot. Of course I thought about what if I had not gone out on that day, beat myself up for not considering what might be slippery, not tying on a safety line. Thoughts of my demise entered my head, as well as worries about my ability to ever have a life like I once did. They were companions I spent a lot of hours with. But as we spoke about earlier, the one edge I had was as someone who had heard from so many people how they had dealt with their traumas, and saw what had worked. I used what I knew. I literally used everything you read about in this chapter on how to deal with my thoughts. Some days one method worked better than another, and other days all I could hold onto was that this was my mind torturing me with a thought, but it was only a thought. I truly had no ability to predict what would happen next, or I would never have been in the situation I was in.

This chapter has introduced you to some of the things we know about thoughts that I have found that can really make a difference. I like the idea of using what works.

"Go to the edge," the voice said.
"No!" they said. "We will fall."
"Go to the edge," the voice said.
"No!" they said. "We will be pushed over."
"Go to the edge," the voice said.
So they went
and they were pushed
and they flew.

- Anonymous

Chapter Nine

Relaxation Skills
Calm Within the Emotional Storm

Joan

Joan had not really taken to the first relaxation exercise. She was a fairly self-conscious person, and the idea of "making faces" while she tensed and relaxed muscles or looking like she was "meditating" was really not her. What if someone walked in on her and saw her sitting in a room with her eyes closed? What would they think? Still she needed to do something, so she stuck with it. Much to her surprise, she found that bit-by-bit, little by little she actually started "getting it". And the more she felt like that, the better she started feeling. Both in general and about the exercises. Her ability to relax deepened, and happened faster and lasted longer over the weeks she practiced. She found despite her original fears about looking silly, that as she gained skills she could actually practice and use the skills just about anywhere! She would practice in her car before she had to go into a meeting with her lawyer (maybe not so much with the facial parts), or in the waiting room at a doctor's appointment (once she dropped the tensing part of the exercises), or just outside over lunch sitting under a tree. It became natural to start looking for places to use it. It actually felt good to get rid of some of that tension.

Then the applications of the relaxation methods came, using the exercises to help with her trauma. It made it a lot easier to have to face her fears, to confront her anxiety if she knew that she was going to be able to quiet some of the storm inside of her that also came when she went to those places or thought those thoughts. She was actually able to sit in her car, collect herself, relax with her thoughts; and then, when ready; to get out of the car and walk past the place where she had been raped! By herself! True it was day time (she was always supposed to stay safe), but still, she never thought she could do that. When the anxiety came, like she had thought it would, she breathed, quieted her muscles, and then walked into her fear. The skills were there. She knew they would be.

After a while, she wasn't sure when, she noticed that she just didn't worry in the same way. Her skills were reliable, and her ability to manage all those feelings had grown. She was getting better, more like the person she wanted to be!

Part of confronting uncomfortable things is the creation of strong physical and emotional reactions. Tension, anxiety, nausea, dizziness, and other feelings can all come when we are remembering or dealing with the aftermath of trauma. The purpose of using relaxation techniques to help at these times has a long history in psychology.

First is the notion of incompatible responses. If you are relaxed, truly relaxed, you cannot be anxious. The nervous system just works that way. But like a lot of things in life, there is the theoretical position and then there is real life. In my experience, you can feel both, but the relaxation skills when properly learned can act like a powerful dimmer switch. They can help you manage better and suffer less.

Second, relaxation skills come in a wide variety of styles, and are easy to teach most people. They can also be taught pretty quickly, taking weeks not years to learn, and for some people they can get significant relief in just days.

Third, if you know you are entering into a place where it's likely to get uncomfortable, wouldn't it be a little easier to go with the knowledge that you aren't going in unarmed? You have some tools or skills that can be used to help you face those things that are about to happen. Relaxation skills have had great success with a lot of situations including specific phobias (like fear of spiders, or heights), test-taking anxiety, social phobias, and for posttraumatic stress responses. Relaxation can be used to help people manage the anxiety that would accompany some of the exposure tasks needed to gain mastery back in those parts of their life.

In our research program at the Center for Stress and Anxiety Disorders in Albany, and in the years of my practice, treatment for anxiety and trauma disorders has often included some type of skill development and experience with progressive muscle relaxation. This is a tried and true technique where people will tense then relax their muscles, helping them to learn how it feels to be tense, to recognize how it feels to be relaxed (physiologically), and then teaching skills that allow these feelings to occur more quickly with great reliability so you can count on them when they are needed. With practice, most people can learn to become deeply relaxed very quickly, in almost any setting. This will become important, because the quicker your ability to apply these skills at those times when you are anxious, like when facing disturbing thoughts or situations, the better the relaxation skill can help you tolerate the situations. The better the situations are tolerated, the longer you can remain in them, and as you've learned earlier, the more completely you can become less responsive or desensitized to those times and places.

We have found that the optimum practice schedule for learning relaxation skills is twice a day. It's certainly possible to practice more often, and you may choose to do that. The reason we say twice per day is optimum is because on average, most people don't report learning deep relaxation any sooner if they practice any more frequently. Learning how to relax takes time, and it requires systematic, regular practice. If you can practice only once a day, or even have to skip a day, that's okay. But remember, it's like any skill, the more you practice the better you'll become, much like playing the piano.

You may have some physical injury or limitations that will make it necessary to adapt the exercise to your particular abilities. That's fine. If as you read or listen to the exercise (you can record the exercises onto your computer, which can then be downloaded to your iPod or other device if you prefer), just don't tense those muscles or an area more than is good for you to do so. Use your own judgment about how hard, if at all, you'd like to tense those muscles. Research has shown that by tensing and then relaxing the muscles, you actually force a physiological change to occur, where the muscles will grow longer (you just stretched them after all) and then quieter. They've become relaxed. It's much like an athlete warming up by stretching the muscles prior to an event.

Relaxation is affected by the setting, although later on once you've learned the skills, you'll be applying them in settings that are far from ideal. But, initially to learn them, we suggest you find a quiet place, safe from intrusion, where you can sit comfortably when you perform the exercises. Be sure that there is support for your head and neck, and if you wear glasses please remove them. When prompted you should try to tense the muscles for about 8-12 seconds, tensing the muscles hard enough to be aware of how they feel when tense, but not so hard as to feel any pain or aggravation. If at any time a muscle hurts, stop what you're doing. The goal is to create enough tension to have a contrast so that the feeling of relaxation stands out as a muscle memory you'll be able to recreate.

Options

The relaxation skills I would like to share here are included in two places: once below, and again online at www.transformingtragedy.com. This is done for a couple of reasons:

First, when reading a book some people like to read from cover to cover, and take in every word. That's fine. However, the exercises listed below are better learned in steps, taking at least 1-2 weeks of twice daily practice to learn the exercises well enough to progress to the next one. To read them in order might be confusing, and put you off. We want to keep you involved, and looking forward to what is coming next. So, this warning is given to help keep some of you on track.

Second, it is often really hard to read an exercise that is generally given verbally, and get the same benefit. That is why an audio version of these exercises is offered as a downloadable option from www.transformingtragedy.com. It's free, and offered as an alternative to the other option which is to read each of the exercises aloud to yourself while making an audio file that you can then store and use on your computer or iPod.

So, with this warning in place, choose the path that works best for you. You may also find it beneficial to skim the exercises in order to have a sense of what can be done. It's up to you. There are no wrong decisions. In my clinical practice, I would have typically gathered a history of the trauma, gone over different types of treatment, and then used part of the 2nd or 3rd treatment session to perform a relaxation exercise, make a copy of the exercise for the patient to use, and provide an overview of how we are going to use the exercises, just like you've been given here.

Relaxation Exercises

The following are three exercises I have used in a variety of applications. The steps are to first use the 11-muscle group relaxation, probably for 2-3 weeks until you feel you're pretty accomplished at it. Then transition into the 4-muscle group relaxation exercise. As you proceed, the exercises become shorter and can be done more quickly with comparable results. Once you've gained skill there, move onto the cued relaxation and relaxation by recall exercise. This exercise allows you to relax by "classical conditioning" where you have used your knowledge of associations to your advantage, pairing the physiological response of relaxation, with a thought or phrase you say in your mind. At that point you should have a really good repertoire of relaxation skills. You can use the skills along the way as you face anxious times or situations, and the skills will be yours for the rest of your life (although like any skill you may find that you may need some practice to get the skills back to where they were when you were well practiced). The ...... punctuation is inserted to indicate there should be a pause. The pause can be anywhere from 5-15 seconds, depending upon what is comfortable for you.

11-muscle relaxation

Muscles used in order of completion:

- Right hand and lower arm
- Right upper arm
- Left hand and lower arm
- Left upper arm
- Forehead and eyes
- Lower face and jaw
- Neck and shoulders
- Chest and upper back
- Abdomen and lower back
- Hips, buttocks, and upper legs (both right and left)
- Lower legs and feet

11-MUSCLE RELAXATION

To begin find a comfortable position. Please be sure to find a place that's comfortable for you to relax in, and a place that will be quiet and you won't be interrupted. To start, gently close you eyes, and take a breath. ....Take a gentle breath in and hold it just for a moment, then relax.... Feel the difference. ....You body tenses slightly as you hold a breath, and then lets go as you exhale. .....Find a rhythm that's right for you. Just letting the air in and out. ......You may find as you relax that your breathing in fact slows down. If it does, just let it happen, and feel the change, as we begin now to focus on the muscles.

Start by making a fist with the right hand. ......Feel the tension in the hand, across the fingers, the thumb, and the wrist, into the lower arm....... Focus on how the tension feels. Notice the tautness in the fingers, the thumb, the wrist. Feel the tension in every fiber. Notice all the tension..... then relax..... Feel the difference. The fingers may tingle and feel warm from the activity. Focus on the change. Some people find the muscles feel warm and heavy as the relaxation enters. ...Some find the muscles grow light as the tension leaves. Notice how it feels for you....., and store those feelings away. Contrast how the muscles felt tight, and how they now feel as the muscles let go. ....Imagine a wave of relaxation has washed up the arm, touching every muscle, deepening the relaxation..... Then imagine the wave is ebbing away, taking with it all the tension. ......Feel the difference, and store those feelings away. ...As we move our attention up now, up to the muscles of the right upper arm.

Raising the right hand up to touch the shoulder, then tense the muscles of the upper arm,.... the bicep and triceps. Feel the tension in these long muscles of the upper arm. Imagine a band or belt has been pulled tight around the upper arm creating tension. Focus on that tension, noticing how every fiber, every muscle feels.... Then relax. ......Feel the difference. Notice the contrast between how the muscles felt tight,.... and how they now feel as they relax....... Imagine that feeling of relaxation has spread up the hand and lower arm, and now is entering the upper arm..... Heavy..... Warm. Focus on the change. Feel that wave of relaxation washing up the arm, and then ebbing away. ... Bringing deep, complete relaxation.... Store those feelings away. Calm.... Quiet.... Focus on the difference between how the muscles felt tight, and how they feel relaxed. Warm, heavy. Allowing these feelings to grow without any thought, we'll move our attention across to the left side, starting with the left hand and lower arm.

Make a fist now with the left hand. Feel the tension in the hand, across the fingers, the thumb, and the wrist, into the lower arm.... Focus on how the tension feels. Notice the tautness again in the fingers, the thumb, and the wrist. ... Feel the tension in every fiber,.. every tension..... then relax. Feel the difference. ...The fingers may tingle and feel warm from the activity. Focus on the change.... Notice how it feels for you, and store those feelings away. ..Contrast how the muscles felt tight, and how they now feel as the muscles let go.... Imagine a wave of relaxation has again washed up the arm, touching every muscle, but now it's on the left side, deepening the relaxation. Then imagine the wave is ebbing away, taking with it all the tension.... Feel the difference, and store those feelings away.... As we move our attention up now, up to the muscles of the upper arm.

Raise the left hand up to touch the shoulder, then tense the muscles of the upper arm, the bicep and triceps..., feel it on this side. Feel the tension in these long muscles of the upper arm. Imagine a band or belt has been pulled tight around the left upper arm creating tension. ....Focus on that tension, noticing how every fiber, every tendon, how every muscle feels.... Then relax. ...Deeply ...feel the difference. Notice the contrast between how the muscles felt tight, and how they now feel as they relax. ....Imagine that feeling of relaxation has spread up the hand and lower arm, and now is entering the upper arm. Heavy. Warm. Focus on the change..... Feel that wave of relaxation washing up the arm, and then ebbing away... Bringing deep, complete relaxation. Store those feelings away. Calm.... Quiet. ...Focus on the difference between how the muscles felt tight, and how they feel relaxed. Warm, heavy... As we move our attention up, up now to the muscles of the face and shoulders.

Here, let's start with the muscles of the forehead and eyes. Begin to press down with the forehead, really tightening the brow, squinting the eyes. Feel all the tension around the eyes,... there's a lot of muscles here that allow us to make all those expressions. .. Feel every muscle, feel the tension on the forehead, pulling on the temple, around the eyes, even pulling the scalp...... then relax. Let all the tension go, and focus on the difference. ..The forehead actually grows longer as it becomes less constricted, more relaxed.... It may tingle and feel warm from all the activity. ..Notice whatever changes are occurring, and store them away. Feel the eyes relax as the tension lets go, and the relaxation deepens and grows. More and more relaxed..... Contrast the feelings from how they felt tight, ... to how they now feel.... relaxed, and calm. Remember those feelings, as we move our attention down, down to the cheeks and jaw.

Here what I'd like you to do is to bite down with your back teeth and pull the corners of your mouth out, making a tight grimace, a really tight face. If possible, I'd also like you to take your tongue and press it into the roof of your mouth or front teeth, Hold that tension, feel where the tightness is.. hold it....then relax. Just let go. Let all the tension leave and focus on the difference. If the jaw is relaxed all the way, it actually hangs open a little bit, as there's not even tension to hold the jaw together. Just let go, ...completely relaxed. And remember those feelings, how it felt tight.....

and how it feels relaxed..... All the muscles of the face relaxing now,.. the forehead... the eyes.... The cheeks....and jaw. Completely relaxed. As we move our attention down, down to the muscles of the neck and shoulders.

Again a caution..., if you've injured any part of your body, don't aggravate the area by tensing the muscles so they hurt. It's not necessary. Just be aware of how tension feels, and more importantly how it feels when the tension goes. That's the memory we want to help you build in.

To start here, gently press you head back, tensing the muscles in the back of the neck. At the same time now, raise your shoulders up, making the muscles feel as if there's a knot, as they work against each other. ..... Hold that tightness, be aware of how the muscles.... feel tight and hard, noticing where the tension is, feeling that tightness...... then relax... Just let go..... Let the head find a comfortable position, just gently resting, no tension holding it up,... and the shoulders just letting go, loose and calm. Sagging.. ....warm and comfortable.... Totally relaxed, again as if that warm comfortable feeling just flows into the area, without any effort at all... as we move our attention down, down now to the muscles of the chest and upper back.

Here we're going to create tension a little bit differently. Here when we start I'd like you to take a breath and hold it, and then relax when you exhale..... When you're ready take a deep breath, hold it, and then tense the muscles of your chest and upper back. Hold it, feel the way the muscles are tight, a lot of tension gets held in this region, ...be aware of how the tightness is felt, where it is, ...then relax, just exhale, and let all the tension out.... Let the next breath in, be a slow, comfortable cleansing breath. Fresh, clean air in... and as you exhale, all the tension leaves. .... Growing calmer, and more deeply relaxed with every breath. Calm... Peaceful...

As we move our attention down, ...down now to the muscles of the stomach and lower back. ...Here as with the chest we're going to tense as we take a breath, hold it, and then relax as we exhale. ....When you're ready take a deep breath, and as you fill your lungs, press your stomach out,... distending it away from the back,... feeling the tightness in the abdomen, the sides of the stomach and even on the lower back. Holding it, feeling the tautness in the muscles, in the whole trunk region ..... then relax.... Just let your breath out and as you do the chest and stomach both collapse, and as you take the next breath, feel the fresh air fill the lungs,....allow the stomach to rise and fall with the chest. ... Easily, effortlessly.... Rising and falling, and with each exhale feel you body sink deeper, and deeper in to the cushions. Just let go. Let all the muscles go limp and loose.... Let the cushions hold you, without any effort.... And as you gently feel your chest and stomach rise, rising much like an infant who breaths without any tension,... feel the relaxation spread into the whole upper body now. ... Calm, peaceful. Deeply relaxed. .... Think the word relax with every exhale, and feel your body just letting go,.... no effort at all, as we move our attention down,... down now to the muscles of the hips and upper legs.

Here, just as when we started, I want you to just tighten and relax the muscles, focusing on the contrast between how the muscles feel tight, and how they feel as you relax........ Start by tightening your hips, your buttock and the muscles of the upper legs, the quads and hamstrings...... Feel the tautness, tighten the hips, the upper legs, feel the tightness, the tension, hold it.... Then relax. ... Just let go..... Feel the change. Again it may feel as if a warm comfortable wave has spread over the muscles, and the tension leaves, as you just sink into the cushions..., imagine the wave of relaxation spreading over the region,... and then as it ebbs away, taking all the tension with it, as we move our attention down, down now to the lower legs and feet.

Start here by curling the toes up, creating tension in the toes, the balls of the feet, the ankles, and the calves on both the right and the left side. ....Hold the tension, feel the tightness, notice how every fiber feels....then let go. ... Just relax completely. .... Imagine all the tension flowing down and out the legs, as the relaxation washes up, ... warm and full, deepening the feeling of calm in every muscle. ..Just letting go, and focusing on the change,... that contrast between tension... and relaxation. ... Store those feelings away. Remember how they feel, and store that muscle memory away....

Now as we've gone through each muscle group once, we're going to go through them a second time. Only this time we're not going to tighten the muscles, just try to relax the muscles that extra little bit, whenever the muscle is mentioned. Starting where we left off, with the muscles of the feet and lower legs, relaxed... quiet.

Now the upper legs and hips.., calm... comfortable..

Stomach and lower back relaxed,.. and breathing calm and peaceful

Chest and upper back, quiet...warm, .. heavy.

Shoulders and neck loose... and calm.

Face, down the forehead, across the eyes....down the cheeks and jaw, loose...heavy.

Then the arms, down the upper arms,... the lower arms... and out the hands and fingers...calm....peaceful

Now, with your mind go through your entire body, focusing on the relaxation...If you feel any muscle group can relax more, try to focus on that group and deepen the relaxation.... no effort, just quiet and calm.. Then, what I'd like you to do is to focus on the next five breaths... Just gently focusing on a gentle, calm breath, and as you exhale count from 1 to 5 for each breath you take, as you inhale, and then, thinking the word relax as you exhale. Noticing yourself growing calmer, and more relaxed with every breath. ....Just take a moment to enjoy those sensations.

In a moment it will be time to come back from this state of relaxation. To do that we'll have you count back in your mind from 3 to 1. With each number, you'll find yourself growing more alert, but still remaining very calm and comfortable. 3 still very calm and comfortable...2, a little more alert, moving around just a bit, growing more aware...and 1 slowly opening your eyes, feeling alert, yet still very calm and peaceful.

You'll find as you practice this exercise the relaxation will deepen and begin to occur sooner with the practice.

4- muscle relaxation

Muscles used and order of completion-

- Both the right and left hands, lower and upper arms
- Feet, legs and buttock (both right and left)
- Abdomen and chest
- Neck and head

4-MUSCLE GROUP RELAXATION

What I would like you to do is to start by finding a comfortable position. Settle down, just close your eyes and take a breath. Fill your lungs with the fresh clean air coming in and when you are ready just gently exhale... Try to find a rhythm to your breathing that is comfortable for you. Just rising and falling.... Very comfortable. ...Begin to think of the word RELAX ...every time you exhale.. and feel the relaxation beginning to spread throughout your body.

We begin the exercise by starting to focus on our hands and arms on both the right and left side. ... What I would like you to do here is to start first by making a fist with your right hand then the left hand, tensing both arms. ... Feel the tension come across the fingers, thumb, wrist and forearm.... Feel the tension all the way up both arms on the right and left side. ... Hold that tension... be very aware of that tension,... holding it,... noticing it,... and notice where all the tightness is held... and then relax. Focus on the difference. ... Focus on the difference between where the tension was and how the relaxation is growing. .... Imagine the relaxation as if a wave that has just washed up the arm,... being a warm and comfortable sensation wherever it touches,...and as it ebbs away taking all the tension with it. Some people find that when the relaxation grows deeper that the arm feels warm and heavy, ...while other people feel that it grows light as the tension leaves. ... Whatever it feels like for you... those are the feelings to store away.

Now we'll move our attention down. Down to the muscles in the lower body.

Here we are going to tense the muscles in the legs, feet, hips and buttocks all at once. ...To do this we will start first by tensing the feet, curl the toes, tense the toes, the balls of your feet, the ankles and calves, right up into the thighs, pressing the legs hard, right into the hips and buttocks, ... pressing down so the whole lower body is made hard and firm. .... Feel the tightness... Be very aware of these sensations, holding it,.. noticing it... and being very aware of where all the tightness is held...... and then relax. ... Just let it go.... As you let it go let all the tension leave.... Let the relaxation enter. ... Again, focus on the difference. ... Feel the relaxation like a warm comfortable wave washing over you,... bringing deep and full relaxation, ...and as it ebbs away ...taking all the tension with it,.... calmer,... quieter... and peaceful. Allow those feelings to deepen and grow..... With the next few breaths every time you exhale feel the relaxation spreading down,..... deeper and deeper relaxed with every breath.

You can move the attention up now to the muscles in the stomach and chest ...... We are going create tension a little differently here. ... We will start first with a good deep breath, then tighten the muscles, hold your breath and relax upon then exhale..... Whenever you are ready take a good deep breath, fill your lungs..... As you fill your lungs then hold the tightness,.... feel the tightness like a band or belt placed around the chest..., hold the tight feeling... tight feeling in the stomach..., tense the muscle in the abdomen, being very aware of all the tension here,... holding the tightness,... being very aware of where the tautness is held and whenever you are ready slowly exhale letting your breath out. ... When you inhale next... imagine the next breath in as a fresh clean cleansing breath. .. As you exhale... just imagine all the tightness leaving. .. Also, notice when you fill the lungs, the stomach rises with the chest... and as you exhale... feel the stomach sink with the chest. Calm...quiet.

Focus on the middle of the trunk now, ...you are breathing now from the diaphragm as the chest and stomach rises as one and as it empties as one. Relax those muscles all the way,... sink deeply into the cushion,.. let all the tension leave; .. let the relaxation grow deeper and deeper. More and more relaxed.... We will come back to this breathing in just a few moments. It is very important that you learn to relax,.. Quieting the chest and stomach by controlling your breathing.

Now we will move our attention up to the muscles in the shoulders, neck, face and scalp.... I would like you to start by pressing your head back, raise the shoulders up, press down the forehead, squint the eyes, and clench the jaw, so all the muscles of the upper region are hard and firm..... Feeling that tightness and being aware of the sensations... and then relax. .. Just let it go.... As you let all the tension leave let the shoulders sag,.. becoming calm and quiet.... The forehead grows smooth.. as the muscles grow longer as they become less constricted, less tense..... You may feel a tingling and a warmth in the muscles, ...whatever you feel.....just focus on those sensations and deepen them... and let them grow... as the relaxation grows deeper and deeper.

We have gone through all the muscles once.... and we will go through them a second time. ... This time we are not going to tighten the muscles. ... I want you to just focus on the muscles trying to relax them... just a little bit more. The forehead, eyes, relaxed.... and calm,.... lower face and jaw... loose,... comfortable. The neck and shoulders... growing relaxed and heavy, ...peaceful, and quiet. The chest and upper back,.... relaxed and breathing calm and quiet. ...... Every time you exhale.... just imagine the relaxation spreading throughout your body. ..... The stomach and lower back,.... just feel the chest and stomach rising... and falling,... calmer and calmer with every breath. ....Hips and upper legs,... relaxed and heavy,.... and the lower legs and feet ..relaxed.... All the tension draining down and out .... as relaxation deepens and grows. The arms,.. down the upper arms, down the lower arms and out the hands and fingers. ....Relaxed and calm.

With your mind now I would like you to go through your body from head to toe or wherever you feel any tension, just try to release the tension even deeper, becoming calmer and quieter, more and more relaxed. Focus on the breathing, rising and falling, filling the lungs very naturally and comfortably. As you relax feel yourself sinking into the cushions, very, very calm, very, very peaceful.

Now,.. what I would like you to do with your mind... is to imagine yourself in a very relaxing place,.. just as completely and vividly as you can, ..I would like you to create that place.... Imagine yourself there now. A warm, comfortable, quiet place....If it is warm, to see the sun and the sky, the color of the sky, clouds or birds,... see the water, smell the water,... hear whether it's just waves or a stream....If you are lying on a beach, to feel the warmth of the sand and grit of it beneath you. .....If you are lying on grass, ..feel the coolness of it. Whatever is there, just create it vividly,... fully with your mind now, enjoy the feelings.... Find a spot or place that is memorable. .. One that is easy to recall. .. Every time you find yourself doing the relaxation exercise and when you become deeply relaxed, ... I would like you to think of this place, that image, or that scene. .... Imagine how deeply relaxed you would be.... Remember those feelings,... remember that contrast,.. how the muscles were tight and now can be so calm, loose . To become more and more relaxed, peaceful, quiet.

Now it is time to come back... as I begin to count backwards from 3 to 1, you'll find yourself growing more alert and awake, yet still calm and comfortable.

When you get to one just slowly open your eyes, coming all the way back.

Three, starting to come out, still very, very comfortable.... Two, a little bit more alert, perhaps moving around just a bit.... One, all the way back, slowly opening your eyes, feeling alert, calm and quiet.

RELAXATION BY RECALL AND CUED RELAXATION

In keeping with the goal of trying to learn briefer, effective relaxation techniques, this section will share two very brief methods for bringing about deep relaxation, quickly. In order to do this, you must first have mastered the prior exercises. Once you feel you are reaching a deep level of relaxation first with the 11muscle group relaxation exercise and then with the 4 muscle group relaxation exercise, its time to learn relaxation by recall.

Relaxation by Recall

First, perform a 4-muscle group relaxation exercise. Once you are comfortably relaxed, go through each muscle group mentally. Try to recall what each group of muscles is like when the muscles are deeply relaxed. Try to have this become a true muscle memory. Recall deep relaxation for the lower body (feet, legs and hips); the trunk (stomach, lower back, chest and upper back), both arms and hands; and the shoulders and face.

If you're able to recall these feelings of relaxation without having to tense the muscles, but by just using recall, congratulations, you have a new tool to use. If you were "pretty successful", continue to supplement the relaxation by recall by performing relaxation with the 4 muscle group exercise until you can get similar feelings with recall alone. If you weren't yet able to produce a deep relaxation feeling by recall alone, don't worry. Keep practicing the earlier exercises, and when you feel ready, try again. Everyone proceeds at their own pace.

Cue-Conditioned Relaxation

The last brief relaxation technique we'd like to share, is called cue-conditioned relaxation. Once the relaxation by recall is going well, you can try to produce relaxation by setting up cues in the environment that are associated with relaxation. First, take a deep breath, and as you exhale, think the word "relax". This should be very familiar to you by now, and can be done at first with your eyes closed, then later with your eyes open.

If you'd like, think of some relaxing imagery to help you relax from head to toe. Once you've done that, your next task is to tie the relaxation to commonly occurring situations in your life. For instance you may find that at a traffic light you can take a breath, exhale, think relax, (keeping your eyes open), and do this every time possible when you're in your car. You can do this exercise every time you take a drink from a cup, or close a document on your computer. If you do this activity over and over, after awhile, it will just occur naturally in a wide variety of situations.

Relaxation skills are best thought of as tools. When and how one uses a tool depends both on the skill of the person using the tool and the task at hand. Be creative in their use. There are dozens of relaxation exercises. Several books are offered in the back of this book, as well as the encouragement to seek out others as your interests and needs guide you.

I use relaxation skills a lot. I like them. In fact I sometimes feel it is almost unfair that as a psychologist I get paid to teach them and use them as I'm teaching them to the people I get to work with. I use them when waiting for my own doctors and dentists. In fact, on one such day, I fell asleep on my physician's examination table as I waited for her to come in for the exam. Relaxation skills are a useful, powerful tool. If you gain sufficient skill, they certainly have a place in how we can deal with the variety of things that life will give us.

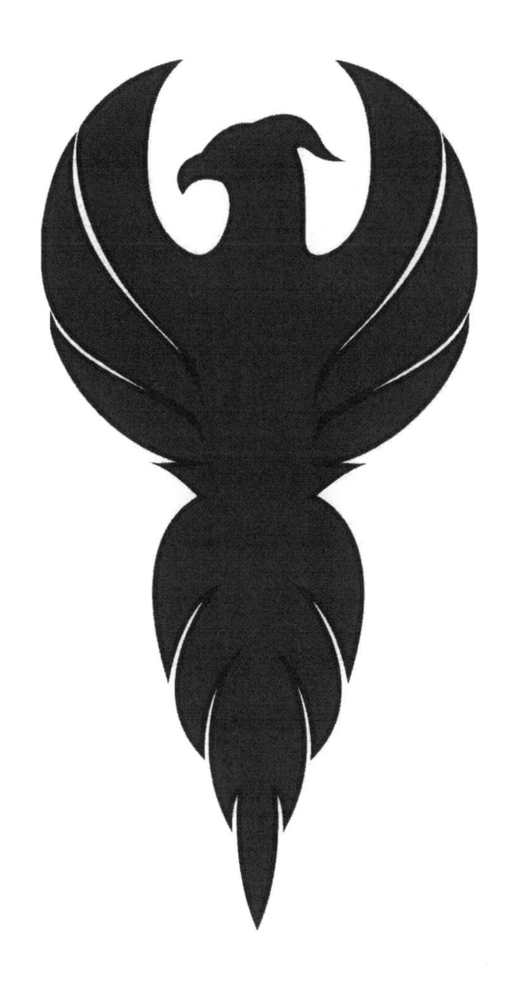

CHAPTER TEN

Mindfulness: How to Show Up in the Present Moment *(Are You Here Now?)*

Otherwise

I got out of bed
on two strong legs.
It might have been
otherwise. I ate
cereal, sweet
milk, ripe, flawless
peach. It might
have been otherwise.
I took the dog uphill
to the birch wood.
All morning I did
the work I love.

At noon I lay down
with my mate. It might
have been otherwise.
We ate dinner together
at a table with silver
candlesticks. It might
have been otherwise.
I slept in a bed
in a room with paintings
on the walls, and

planned another day
just like this day.
But one day, I know,
it will be otherwise.

- Jane Kenyon

Tied to the notion of how our mind works, and how we either do well or do not do well following life's traumas, is the notion of living in the present. As we've heard in all of the previous chapters, when we get caught up in how things were (the past) and our regrets and ideas about the past that lead to pain, or if we leave the present to think about the future and get caught in the worries about what might happen, or how things in our minds will turn out (generally for the worse), we have left the present moment. Our mind has taken us into a place of thoughts; of creating stories that have the capability of hooking us and leading us to a place of great pain.

This concept is shared in Rousseau's description of happiness from his "Reveries of a Solitary Walker":

"If there is a state where the soul can find a resting-place secure enough to establish itself and concentrate its entire being there, with no need to remember the past or reach into the future, where time is nothing to it, where the present runs on indefinitely but this duration goes unnoticed, with no sign of the passing of time, and no other feeling of deprivation or enjoyment, pleasure or pain, desire or fear than the simple feeling of existence, a feeling that fills our soul entirely, as long as this state lasts, we can call ourselves happy, not with a poor incomplete and relative happiness

such as we find in the pleasures of life, but with a sufficient, complete and perfect happiness which leaves no emptiness to be filled in the soul."

Or in the following poem by Michael Chitwood:

Here I Am, Lord

The ribbed black of the umbrella
is an argument for the existence of God,

that little shelter
we carry with us

and may forget
beside a chair

in a committee meeting
we did not especially want to attend.

What a beautiful word, umbrella.
A shade to be opened.

Like a bat's wing, scalloped.
It shivers.

A drum head
beaten by the silver sticks

of rain
and I do not have mine

and so the rain showers me.

So, as countless authors, philosophers and teachers show us, we struggle to live in the present. Why would this be so important for those of us following trauma? Well, even if it's been made clear, it merits being said again: the very nature of a trauma is it will grab us and make it hard to move forward. Our mind wants to make sense of things that don't make sense. It cries out to do so. It is our mind again that replays the events over and over, searching for clues that can help us find order and understanding to things that don't make sense. And once there, any future is colored in a way that makes it all too easy to seem dark and without hope.

So if we are instructed to be mindful, what exactly does that mean, and how can you do that? Mindfulness is a very simple yet complicated idea at the same time. It is a very old and wonderful technique for helping us return to the moment. Mindfulness, simply put, as described by one of the true leaders in this area, Jon Kabat-Zinn, is paying attention, on purpose, in the present moment, non-judgmentally.

Think about that for a second. Basically you're not trying to change anything. You're just trying to be aware. You're doing it willfully and you're not allowing thoughts about the past or the future to take over and you're doing it without judging. Each of these is hard to do. It's easy to say, "That's a good thought. That's a bad thought. I shouldn't be doing that." That's you having thoughts and judgments. Try to place them aside. When you find yourself thinking about where you'd rather be later, what you might have done earlier, return to the present moment. Breathe. You're also NOT trying to relax. That may or may not occur. Awareness is being open to whatever is there, and accepting it without struggling.

The following exercises and text are here to help open this door for you.

Breathing in, I calm my body
Breathing out, I smile.
Dwelling in the present moment
I know this is a wonderful moment.

- Thich Nhat Hanh

Mindful Breathing

Begin by sitting with your feet flat on the floor, back straight, head comfortable, either closing your eyes, or fixing them on a spot on the floor. Bring your attention to your breathing, and observe it, as if you've never really noticed breathing before.....Notice how air enters, through the mouth or nose...and then goes down, deeply into your lungs..... Notice as it flows back out again. It might be slightly warmer as it goes out.......and slightly cooler as it enters. Notice the other things occurring... the rise and fall of your shoulders.....and your chest.......and perhaps even the soothing rise and fall of your abdomen. Fix your attention on these areas. Try to keep your attention on one of these areas, whichever one you prefer, the air going in and out, the chest rising and falling, or the abdomen in its rising and falling.

Keep your attention on the in and out of the breath.................. Whatever urges, feelings, or other sensations come, whether pleasant or unpleasant, gently acknowledge them. And let them be. Allowing yourself just to watch, as you keep your attention on your breath....... Each time your attention may wander, as it gets caught up in thoughts, sounds, notice what it was that distracted you, and bring your attention back to your breath ......No matter how often you drift off, you are simply to notice where you drifted, notice what distracted you, and come back and refocus on your breath............Again, and again you'll drift off into your thoughts. This is normal and natural and happens to everyone. Our minds distract us from what we are doing. So, each time your mind drifts off, notice it, acknowledge it, accept it..........If you find frustration, impatience, boredom, anxiety or other feelings arise, again just notice them, and label them for what they are, and refocus back to your breath.

You may be aware of sounds in the room where you are, or sounds outside. If so, again acknowledge them, and gently bring yourself back, to refocus once again on your breath........When you are ready, gently reopen your eyes, and bring yourself fully back to the room.

The exercise can be recorded by you, or a similar exercise is downloadable from the web site: www.transformingtragedy.com

Mindful awareness can occur anywhere. To be fully aware as you do the dishes, or when walking, are traditional meditational, mindfulness exercises. The goal is to always try to focus on a task, notice those things that interfere, and accept; do not try to force the process. You are learning to be present; to be an observer of what is actually taking place. Not letting those things inside of you take you to places where you didn't intend to go. Thoughts are thoughts. You will learn how to either follow them or not. That which you can observe is meant to be the guide in your life, not all the voices or feelings that have led you to places you didn't want to go.

A simple, but enjoyable exercise is to try to eat something with mindfulness, such as an orange:

With this being your focus, begin by picking up the orange. Notice the texture. Notice the color, and if there is a fragrance you might already be aware of. Take your time. If you find you are hurrying, and this is because there are thoughts distracting you from the task, notice them, and then refocus on the thing you wanted to do, to mindfully eat the orange. You wanted the full experience, without the distractions that would take away any portion of the experience. Begin to peel the orange. What is that like? How does it feel to pull the skin away? What smell fills the air? Are there bits of pulp you notice and choose to pull away as well? Slowly take it all in. When you're ready, pull a piece of orange away from the whole. Did any juice drip on you? How does that feel if it happened? Slowly raise the piece you've picked and smell it. Act like a connoisseur. When you're ready place the piece of orange into your mouth, and bite. Experience how it feels. Did anything distract you? Or were you able to fully appreciate the taste. How your teeth felt, your tongue. The juices and how it felt, as you were able to swallow and take it in. All the way down. And then another. Until finally the orange is gone. Fully eaten and experienced.

- Russ Harris

Many people gain great benefit from use of the mindfulness exercises. As you have been shown, if you're here, and not caught up in the impossible ways of solving things in the past or future, you're already in a better place to deal with what is really troubling you; feelings, thoughts, worries, sensations and experiences that are here right now. Finally, you're in a position where you can deal with them.

A useful metaphor that describes this is that of *trying to drive a car while looking in the rearview mirror*. The rearview mirror *shows where you've been*. It might have been a terrible place, full of danger and things that demanded your full attention. Then. But if you try to drive your car only looking there, what is likely to happen? It certainly makes it hard to arrive where you'd like to go, as you're not able to focus on it, and in fact if you kept all the attention on the past, a crash is pretty likely. The goal then is to get one's attention where it needs to be, here in the present, focusing on what can and needs to be accomplished.

A Momentary Creed

I believe in the ordinary day
that is here at this moment and is me

I do not see it going its own way
but I never saw how it came to me

it extends beyond whatever I may
think I know and all that is real to me

it is the present that it bears away
where has it gone when it has gone from me

the only presence that appears to stay
everything that I call mine is lent me

even the way that I believe the day
for as long as it is here and is me

- W.S. Merwin

Acceptance and Commitment Therapy (ACT)

One of the more recent approaches in psychological treatment, including the treatment of trauma, is included in the latest wave of cognitive behavioral therapy. This approach does not subscribe to the belief that the intention of treatment is to change the symptoms of PTSD, but rather it is to help the person *Accept* and move forward to those things in life that matter most, even with the symptoms, whether they continue or not. Remember in an earlier chapter when we spoke about pleasant events scheduling, a related notion was offered that was to not wait until you feel better to do something, but to do that something whether you felt the way you wanted or not. Acceptance and Commitment Therapy (or ACT said as one word) has taken this approach and a whole lot more.

ACT begins with the idea that while symptom reduction occurs, this is a by product not a goal, of the intervention. It instead begins with the idea of ACCEPTING the unwanted, private experiences, which are out of your personal control, and COMMITTING with action to move towards things that each individual defines as a valued life. So, to quote one of the leading ACT proponents, Russ Harris, "The aim of ACT is to create a rich, full and meaningful life, while accepting the pain that inevitably goes with it".

There was an article about a woman whose husband experienced short-term memory loss due to a traumatic brain injury he suffered from falling off their sleeping loft. Under the illusion that her husband would heal, she described being in a crisis mode for the entire first year, devoting herself exclusively to his care and dropping everything else. Convinced that devotion would cure him, she felt she could offer him no less. But as it became gradually clear that his impairment was permanent, she changed her goal from healing him to creating for both of them, as satisfying a life as possible. She knew that for that to succeed, she needed to be honest about, and accept what both of them needed in their lives in order to thrive.

- Anonymous

ACT is a psychological treatment, that adds to our understanding of how to deal with our thoughts and experiences, especially those thoughts and experiences we spend so much time struggling with, and wish we could banish from our existence.

In addition to the use of mindfulness, ACT therapists address the mind, by which they actually mean the language that is involved in how we think, compare, analyze, judge, visualize, etc., all of which are uniquely human. Language (and thoughts) allow us to make maps of the external world, predict what will happen next, share our insights and knowledge, learn from the past, create new things, and carry a history which allows us to deal effectively with things in the world. On the down side, language allows us to try to deal with our internal experiences in similar ways, even though the rules internally may not and often are not the same. What works on the outside to get us food or keep us alive, doesn't work so well on the inside, or at controlling uncontrollable things like our private thoughts, feelings and internal experiences.

So, our ability to think, to create narratives, to imagine things, to compare things has advantages, and disadvantages. The ACT therapist often approaches treatment with questions such as, "What have you done so far? and "What has worked to help solve your problems?" Many times people struggle to control things that are uncontrollable, such as feelings and thoughts that just pop into their head (Remember the elephant? "Twinkle twinkle, little ____ ?"). Since control is seen as the problem, not the symptoms that arise (e.g., anxiety, unwanted feelings), ACT attempts to help people see the futility of continuing down a road that doesn't lead to where they can arrive (i.e. to be free of uncontrollable feelings and thoughts). ACT instead teaches ways to accept and move with those things that are causing someone to limit their life, and through experiential methods, show how our thoughts, and feelings and internal experiences can be dealt with in a way that doesn't require so much struggle.

This means helping people learn what thoughts are; thoughts, nothing more, nothing less. You are not your thoughts. Thoughts are merely sounds, stories, bits of language, passing through our head. You can pay attention if they are helpful, or call them what they are if we can't put them down, thoughts – nothing more or nothing less. Whether something is working for you is a big question in this approach.

So, one approach is to watch thoughts as an experience, with you as an observer of that experience. Learning to look at thoughts, rather than from your thoughts, builds in some space to allow the real you, the person who is able to watch yourself have thoughts and thereby begin the process to act more the way you would like to act. ACT spends time showing how we can get caught up in judgments and thoughts that greatly impact how we view ourselves, and what we can and can't do at those times.

As I said, ACT is more an experiential approach than simply a talking approach. So let's illustrate this approach with two exercises:

The first exercise is to imagine a game of chess. Now in chess the game takes two players, each has a team with pieces. When one player makes a move, the other player then makes a counter move. The goal is to outsmart the other player by making better moves and thereby to win the game. So, imagine you are playing the game. But in this game, the black pieces are the thoughts that make up your anxieties, worries and fears, and everything that could trigger those reactions. The white pieces represent your counter moves, the things you can do to counter the anxieties, worries and fears (the way you think or things that you could do). So, when the black player attacks with a piece (such as a thought that "I'm going to never get better!"), you get on the back of one of your players, ride into the battle on one of your white pieces and counter with the thought, "I'll be alright. I just need to use my medicine like I was told". Then the black player attacks again, with a thought like "That only works some of the time, and this is not the time!" to which you and the white piece counter, "Then I'll add in some deep breathing as well". And back and forth it goes. The real problem here is that rather than having two players, the two opposing players are really one team, YOU! So all of the thoughts, the negative and the positive, all belong to you. And you know each move before it even happens. So the game is fixed. No matter which side wins that particular game, one part of you is the loser. So, when it is your own thoughts and feelings competing against each other, it's a war that inevitably can't be won, and will continue forever. This of course would leave you feeling hopeless, and probably wondering what it is these ACT therapists are trying to do.

- (Hayes et al 1999)

What this exercise is trying to do is to show that if you got a different perspective, maybe you'd see that the pieces aren't really you; yes they are your thoughts, but the real you is the board. This is also an important role, because as a board you don't have to take sides. Games are won by white; games are won by black. The board sees it all without taking sides. If you were a player all those anxieties, worries and fear would matter. But the board doesn't care, or see winners or losers. It just provides the space for the game and lets it happen. Being a board changes a lot of things. You don't have a stake in the outcome, and then you can be an impartial observer.

A second exercise is one where you can simply learn about thoughts and feelings by watching them occur, and learning how to be a good observer of what your mind is doing:

First, get into a comfortable position in either a chair or lying down. Try not to cross your arms or legs, and get as comfortable as possible. Take a few moments to get in touch with the movements of your body. Feel the movement of your breath and the sensations of your body. Feel the chest rising and falling. Feel any warmth or coolness on your skin, where perhaps your foot touches the floor if you're sitting, or where you back touches a cushion if lying down. Notice any rhythm in your body, and any physical sensations. There's no need to control your breathing in any way, just let what happens, happen and be aware.

Now, with your eyes closed, I'd like you to visualize that you're sitting in a very special place. It's somewhere familiar to you, perhaps when you were younger. And on that special day long ago, or perhaps more recently in your own life, with your kids, or a friend, you had one of those simple wands and a bottle of soapy solution that when you dipped the wand inside you could make wonderful bubbles. Some large, some small, sometimes several. Sometimes many. Other times just one. They are all different in size and as the light hits them they appear so many different ways. As you imagine this happening, I'd like you to allow yourself to relax inside and just watch for a bit. And then, when you're willing, I'd like you to go inside yourself and notice what's there. As you look there you will notice all sorts of things; thoughts, feelings, sensations. Just notice them, and give each a label. Pay attention, observe, and then allow yourself to see them as if you could almost see them written in your mind. There might be thoughts like "This is stupid", or "Am I doing this right?".

Just label them as thoughts, and as they occur, gently place them on, or even inside of a bubble. It's kind of interesting, each thought goes on or in a bubble. The bubble can float or get weighed down. It can hover and stay for awhile. They might rise up and either pop, or just disappear. Each does what it does, takes as long as it takes, until it is replaced by the next one. Just continue doing this for a bit longer...

Interesting. How you can be there watching your thoughts like this. Then, when you're ready, begin to come back. Growing aware of the sounds around you. No longer outside, just sitting where you sit. And still you can see the thoughts as thoughts, feelings as feelings, sensations as sensations. Aware of how it feels to sit where you sit. There may be sounds outside you're growing aware of also. Just notice them and label them for what they are. Then when you're ready just open your eyes, and come all the way back. Aware that if you try, you can do this very same act anywhere, to be aware of the thoughts and experiences inside of you, and how you don't need to feed, or get attached to those feelings, just letting them occur, without judging them, or acting upon them, whatever they are.

- www.transformingtragedy.com

ACT allows one to take the response and pull apart thoughts and deal with reactions, emotions and behaviors in a way that lets you see them for what they are and nothing more.

"In the beginner's mind there are many possibilities, but in the expert's there are few."

- Shunryu Suzuki, *Zen Mind, Beginner's Mind*

Cognitions, or thoughts, color all of our lives. The key is to help people stay in the here and now. To be present is something that we will talk about more in the following chapters. It is very difficult to do. But if you just take that concept, "regrets from the past", and think about what's in the now, the thoughts and memories of the trauma can be dealt with somewhat differently. The tragic events that happened and all the thoughts tied up there - what could have been, what happened, things that went wrong, the pain that's there and how that pulls you back, or the worries about the future, how I'm not going to get better, how things won't change, how this is forever going to be, none of those things truly exist. They're ideas in our head that cause great suffering and pain. One approach, mindfulness, as you're learning in Chapter 10, leads to us being here and now fully, and is another skill that has great application.

There is an old saying, *"Men make plans and God laughs."*

I think this idea about how we spend so much time making plans in an effort to control uncontrollable things applies to a lot of situations, but here it certainly makes great sense. We think many things. We think, "if only I'd done this or that", but in truth we have very little power over these things. We just very much want to have this control, and thinking about this is one of the ways that we do this. Unfortunately, as ACT shows us, we truly have to form a different relationship with our pasts and our internal states if we are to live a valued and meaningful existence.

When I was in the trauma center as a patient I used mindfulness often. When I was faced with fears of what could happen, I made clear decisions about what I was going to say and do to those around me. There was a type of mantra I used which kept bringing me back to the present, which was, "This is the most important moment in my life". It was. When you don't know how many moments you have left, and are fully aware of that fact, it made a difference to me if I said something nice to the orderly who roughly transported me to the gurney, or how I responded to the nurse who didn't respond to my call bell because my jaw was wired shut and it was hard to speak. But while it would have been easy to get mad, I really didn't want those to be the last words I would be remembered for. Also, I believed how I responded might make a big difference in how I might be treated the next time that nurse was needed, or the orderly was lifting me onto an x-ray or other cold, hard machine. So I tried to say things that helped build those moments to be the way I wanted them to be. I tried to be nice. I tried to understand not just me, but them, as best as I could. Trying my best to do that, in the pain, in the drug filled haze at times, and in the anxiety and worry I frequently held.

There was one night when I was placed on a morphine pump to manage my pain following surgery. The theory is that since I was post op, if the pain got bad, rather than wait until the next time a pill could be given, I was in charge of my medication, so I could stay comfortable and not take more or less than I needed. Unfortunately, that night I was in terrible pain. I pushed the button (which was hard to do given my broken bones and placement of the button), but it never brought any relief. When the nurse came in she checked to make sure it was working, and said there was nothing more she could do. So for that night, I was awake with my pain, in a dark hospital bed, all alone with all that was going on inside of me: pain, fear, worry. I used mindfulness (and some relaxation) to keep my focus on what was occurring. I couldn't escape the pain as much as I wanted to, and there was no way to get any relief. The next morning the surgeon came and asked how the night went. I told him how it had gone, and he couldn't understand. The pump was there to help, at which time his nurse practitioner chimed in blaming me for holding my broken arm which they had operated on in a poor position and thereby inflicting the pain upon myself. I firmly let them know that it didn't matter what they thought, I was in pain and needed something different.

At that point they conceded the point and let me know the anesthesiologist would be up later. When he finally arrived 3 hours later, he discovered that even though the pump looked like it had been dispensing medicine when the button was pushed, not one drop of medicine had been given. The machine had been broken and giving false readings. So for nearly 24 hours since the operation to reconstruct my crushed right wrist, I hadn't received any pain medication at all. If not for the mindfulness exercises, which in this case needed to make room for a great deal of pain, as well as everything else, I fully believe it would have been an even worse night.

"There is a story of a woman running away from tigers. She runs and runs, and the tigers are getting closer and closer. When she comes to the edge of a cliff, she sees some vines there, so she climbs down and holds on to the vines. Looking down, she sees that there are tigers below her as well. She then notices that a mouse is gnawing away at the vine to which she is clinging. She also sees a beautiful little bunch of strawberries close to her, growing out of a clump of grass. She looks up and she looks down. She looks at the mouse. Then she just takes a strawberry, puts it in her mouth, and enjoys it thoroughly.

Tigers above, tigers below. This is actually the predicament that we are always in, in terms of our birth and death. Each moment is just what it is. It might be the only moment of our life, it might be the only strawberry we'll ever eat. We could get depressed about it, or we could finally appreciate it and delight in the preciousness of every single moment of our life."

- Pema Chodron

We can often get pulled by our minds into things that we are still carrying from the past (such as regrets, "what if's", should's, or other emotionally charged memories). They take us away from "now". The same is what happens when our mind begins to worry or think about the future. Planning is a good thing. We can sometimes make plans that help us deal with things that actually come to pass. Many things we think about, especially our worries when they are unfounded, only cause us distress and pain. Being in the present brings us back to where we actually live, in the moment.

Or, as Yogi Berra said, *"The future ain't what it used to be" and "You can observe a lot by watching".*

The following is a well-known story that can give us pause. While we couldn't locate the author, it is readily available on the Internet. Please read it, and then just let it leave whatever impact it may:

Imagine...

There is a bank that credits your account each morning with $86,400.

It carries over no balance from day to day. Every evening deletes whatever part of the balance you failed to use during the day.

What would you do? Draw out ALL OF IT, of course!

Each of us has such a bank. Its name is TIME

Every morning, it credits you with **86,400 seconds**. Every night it writes off, as lost, whatever of this you have failed to invest to good purpose. It carries over no balance. It allows no overdraft.

Each day it opens a new account for you. Each night it burns the remains of the day. If you fail to use the day's deposits, the loss is yours. There is no going back. There is no drawing against the "tomorrow".

You must live in the present on today's deposits. Invest it so as to get from it the utmost in health, happiness, and success! The clock is running. Make the most of today.

To realize the value of **ONE YEAR**, ask a student who failed a grade.

To realize the value of **ONE MONTH**, ask a mother who gave birth to a premature baby.

To realize the value of **ONE WEEK**, ask the editor of a weekly newspaper.

To realize the value of **ONE HOUR**, ask the lovers who are waiting to meet.

To realize the value of **ONE MINUTE**, ask a person who missed the train.

To realize the value of **ONE SECOND**, ask a person who just avoided an accident.

To realize the value of **ONE-TENTH OF A SECOND**, ask the person who won a silver medal in the Olympics.

Treasure every moment that you have! And treasure it more because you shared it with someone special to spend your time with. And remember that time waits for no one.

Yesterday is **history**. Tomorrow is a **mystery**.

Today is a gift. That's why it's called the **present**!

Chapter Eleven

Writing Our Stories
The Power of the Pen and Personal Narratives

Mona

Mona had kept a journal forever. As a little girl it was filled with the details of her every day life, her friends, her family, birthdays, holidays and thoughts about personal events or ideas that she liked seeing in writing. But after the rape, she stopped writing in the journal. It was just too hard to face the words on the page, and to relive the anguish she went through every time she was reminded of what had happened. So, she was more than a little surprised, and reluctant when her therapist asked her to write out what happened to her. She had thought the sessions had been going fairly well. True things were not getting that much better, but she wasn't feeling worse either. But after a lot of cajoling and pushing, she agreed. Mona was a person of her word, so she did what she had agreed to, to write down her memories of that night, including the thoughts, feelings, sensations as best as she could recall. It was hard. It took almost 6 days to actually do it, and if there wasn't a scheduled appointment the next day she would have delayed it even longer. When she entered the session that day, a strange thing happened. She was asked to read what she had written out loud. That wasn't what she had agreed to! But she liked her therapist, and after some more encouragement, she agreed to try. The words were hard to form. They brought up such strong emotion it surprised even her. After all she had written those words, why would saying them out loud be so powerful? The next surprise was she was asked to read them again, and again. Each time to pause, to breathe and to allow whatever feelings and thoughts came from the reading to just be there. By the end of the session the reaction was a lot less. Surprising. When she was asked to continue her writing, adding in more details and memories as they came, she wasn't excited about doing that, but felt hope that you know what, this might actually help!

Exposure to things one doesn't want to face, or those things that provoke unwanted feelings related to a trauma, need to be addressed and resolved, if one is to move on. That is the state of our current knowledge, and a part of all of the scientifically sound treatments for PTSD at this time. In our Albany MVA treatment project, we did this in a number of ways, but one central way was to have people write about what happened to them. They were instructed to write a very complete description of the trauma, which included the details of what happened as best as they knew, where it happened, what their thoughts were as it was going on, as well as any other memories such as images, sights, sounds, smells and details which may have seemed insignificant or left out up to this point. They were instructed to try to keep the description in a chronological order, paying particular attention to their thoughts and feelings (both emotional and physical). They were to describe what led up to the moment, what then occurred, and what happened afterward. They were to try to keep the length of the description between 2 -3 pages long. Too short, and there isn't enough to work with, too long and people tend to get bogged down in the length and not work as well as more targeted pieces. They were not to worry about grammar or complete sentences, but rather to get it down on paper in whatever way they could. Some people might be able to do it in one setting; others might only be able to do it in smaller doses. There was no right or wrong way to do it, but if agreeable they were to do it between our sessions and bring it with them the next time we met.

Once we met, the description was then read aloud. The reading was discussed along with any thoughts, feelings and reactions that occurred in that moment. They were then addressed with the tools you've been learning about, addressing the thoughts, making room for the feelings, and using relaxation to quiet some of the upset. Then they were asked to read it again. And again. And again. Until the feelings became less. Session length didn't matter; what mattered was guiding someone through the experience in a way that would be helpful.

An adaptation of the form is included below:

My Trauma Description

Write or type a two-to-three page description of your trauma. Be sure to include a chronological account of the traumatic event, including what happened and what you saw, felt, heard, and smelled. Be sure to include the date, the events that led up to the trauma, what you experienced, as well as any thoughts or images that might stand out.

Our intent was to help with exposure. We had each person read the description 3-4 times each day, and then incorporate any new thoughts or changes into the evolving description. Over time, as hoped, the reactions became less and less; and at some point the reading, both in session and outside on their own time, was stopped. The upset that had initially followed was gone, and the need to avoid those memories abated. They were not gone. No one can take away the memories. But our intent was to make carrying them a little easier.

If you remember back to some of the theories of PTSD, one reason trauma memories remain and are so powerful is that the memories are fragmented, and well incorporated into our way of thinking and perceiving ourselves and our world. Writing forces organization of material. It also provides clear material to look at, in a very concrete way, which can lead to new ways to see and carry the material.

The use of writing has been a part of a number of other similar psychological interventions. In some of those studies, such as the ones using Cognitive Processing Therapy (CPT, a very good treatment for PTSD), the active treatment elements were "dismantled" to see how much less of an impact you would get, if you were only given a part of the treatment (the cognitive part, or the writing part). Or another way is to ask, do we need to give the whole, complicated treatment to get equally good results? Findings from these studies supported the powerful role writing can have. In fact, while the combined treatment was best, if you could only use part of the treatment they had put together, and you weren't a highly trained cognitive therapist, use the writing part!

Which is not surprising, given that there is considerable research that writing about difficult, even traumatic experiences, has been found for years to improve not just mood, but also one's physical well being. It seems that the use of writing, either in a therapeutic way, or in the privacy of a journal or diary, can have profound positive effects. Interested readers can find references for this in the appendix if they'd like to learn more.

But wait, we haven't finished with this topic yet. The use of writing following traumas is something you don't have to wait to do.

The Personal Narrative Workbook: Transforming Tragedy by a Directed Program of Confrontation and Meaning

As we've already discussed, writing about trauma has been used in several important ways.

First, as a type of exposure, Second as a stand alone type of treatment, helping people organize, make tangible the impact of trauma, and Third, to study the overall psychological benefits of writing on both psychological and medical well being.

In Europe, writing, or an internet based therapy termed "interapy", used writing as an online treatment for PTSD.

The following is a treatment using writing I have developed and used in my own practice to complement or serve as an adjunctive treatment for survivors of trauma. It is described here to illustrate how some of the things you're learning can shape the ways we can creatively use that knowledge. The exercises are listed sequentially. To do the exercise, you need to do them in order, and not move too fast into the next one. The number of repetitions are simply recommendations, not any hard and fast rule. Please read through them all, and see where the exercise is leading you. If you think it would be helpful, please begin with the first one, and see where it takes you.

Exercise One

What we'd like you to do at this time is to write out a description of your traumatic event(s). Try to make it as personal as possible (use "I", and other first person descriptions), write it in a chronological order, and try to include your subjective experience more than just facts. Be sure to include thoughts, feelings, memories, fears, and any other description that would help make it as thorough as you can make it at this time.

We have had patients do this for the past decade. We have learned that it is not necessary that the written description be a prize-winning essay. In fact, it does not even require complete sentences; phrases will do. It is important, however, to remember the details of your trauma as best as you can. This description of the trauma becomes a very important way to help you regain your life and to deal with the thoughts and intrusions that are problematic. This will become a tool for you to use.

We understand that this is often a difficult assignment. Some people can only do this a little bit at a time, writing just short passages about parts of the trauma. Other people write at great length and then try to forget about what they wrote as fast as they can. It would be expected at this point that you might want to avoid, or escape from something that makes you feel bad, even if you are now becoming aware of how it will eventually help you. If this task takes several attempts to complete, so be it. You need to start with whatever you can do, and then build upon that as best you can. Writing this description and facing the memories is a very courageous act. We believe this task will help you begin the process of returning to the way you were or where you would like to be.

NOTE: This is based upon the exposure you did in an earlier chapter. If you already did that, use that version. If you didn't do that exercise, here is one of the new variations we've come up with since.

My Trauma Description

What we'd like you to do at this point is to write or type a 2-3 page description of your traumatic event. Be sure to include a chronological account of the trauma, what happened, what you saw, felt, heard, and smelled (the date, what led up to it, what you went through and what happened), as well as any thoughts or images that stand out. Write in the first person (I) and especially write about those areas that have been hard to deal with or face for too long.

Ok get some paper and begin writing.

Read and re-read 3-4x/day for 7-10 days.

Exercise Two

Ok, now what we'd like you to do is to look at the description you've written in the first exercise as something to critique. We'd like you to see if there are ideas there that are powerfully portraying a certain view of yourself, the world or your future that take place. People who are stuck following a trauma seem to ruminate over the event rather than learn a way to process it, to help reintegrate it into their own life. This time however, we want you to use the worksheets that follow on how to deal with thoughts and how to foster resilience, and try to apply it as it makes sense for you, in your description. You may want to think of how a really good friend, who had gone through a similar event may have responded, and how they would advise you.

My Trauma Description

What we'd like you to do at this point is to write or type a 2-3 page description of your traumatic event. Be sure to include a chronological account of the event, what happened, what you saw, felt, heard, and smelled (the date, what led up to it, what you went through and what happened), as well as any thoughts or images that stand out. This time however, we want you to use the list of how people get unstuck, and try to apply it as it makes sense for you, in your description. You may want to think of how a really good friend, who had gone through a similar event may have responded, and how they would advise you.

Ok get some paper and begin writing.

Read and re-read 3-4X/day.

Worksheet for Second Exercise of Personal Narrative

How you think about the trauma is powerful. One major finding about who moves through traumatic events and who remains stuck is held in the idea of how one thinks about what happened.

People who have had a tragic event occur often ruminate, or think about the event over and over without ever reaching any resolution. Sometimes that's because there can't be resolution (e.g. "Why did this happen?"), and sometimes because they can't think about it in a way that let's them move on ("I need to escape the awful feelings that the memories bring up").

There are several major areas of change in thinking that have been helpful for some people:

The first is how the world now looks as a result of what happened. It often now seems that the world is more dangerous, and our ideas about safety, fairness, and how we expect things to happen are greatly challenged. It is easy to leap to the idea that, "The world is very dangerous, and I have no control over anything", or "I can't tolerate the painful emotions related to my trauma". These are powerful ideas. Maybe the world is as dangerous as it ever was (no more and no less), but you now see it as more dangerous than it truly is. Or maybe you can control some things, not necessarily how your thoughts pop into your head, but what you do with them (i.e. deal with them, see them as thoughts, not as necessarily truth, but as an idea). Maybe you have been through a lot and in fact, while the experience may have been unpleasant and hard, you are able to deal with a lot, even pain and feelings you never experienced before.

How trauma is seen is important (is it time limited or protracted? Does it seem as if it will never end?). People, who do well see the trauma as an event, which while hard, is an event that will not last forever. You are here. Now. The event is past. You have hope.

Trauma memory is often not well organized, unlike other memories we've had in our lives. That's one of the reasons why writing about the trauma, like you did in the first exercise, in organizing that memory of the event chronologically, looking at what happened, what we felt, thought, and did, can help it become like other memories.

The bad feelings and aftermath however, often make this a very difficult suggestion to follow.

Avoidance of these unpleasant feelings, or places, people or things that provoke us make us want to get away or escape these reminders of what happened. Unfortunately, like trying to hold down a ball under water, the more you try to do so, the harder the ball wants to pop to the surface. Our thoughts are like that.

To get over bad experiences one unfortunately needs to spend some time with these bad feelings and memories. Hopefully not too much. But enough to help the feelings get managed, made smaller and less powerful. So, the writing has been one big step in this direction.

The worksheet from the APA on how to build resilience is included once again, as an aid if you wanted to use those points as suggestions or new ways to deal with the memories and your life.

10 Ways to Build Resilience

1) **Make connections.** Good relationships with close family members, friends, or others are important. Accepting help and support from those who care

about you and will listen to you strengthens resilience. Some people find that being active in civic groups, faith-based organizations, or other local groups provides social support and can help with reclaiming hope. Assisting others in their time of need also can benefit the helper.

2) **Avoid seeing crises as insurmountable problems.** You can't change the fact that highly stressful events happen, but you can change how you interpret and respond to these events. Try looking beyond the present to how future circumstances may be a little better. Note any subtle ways in which you might already feel somewhat better as you deal with difficult situations.
3) **Accept that change is a part of living.** Certain goals may no longer be attainable as a result of adverse situations. Accepting circumstances that cannot be changed can help you focus on circumstances that you can alter.
4) **Move toward your goals.** Develop some realistic goals. Do something regularly -- even if it seems like a small accomplishment -- that enables you to move toward your goals. Instead of focusing on tasks that seem unachievable, ask yourself, "What's one thing I know I can accomplish today that helps me move in the direction I want to go?"
5) **Take decisive actions.** Act on adverse situations as much as you can. Take decisive actions, rather than detaching completely from problems and stresses and wishing they would just go away.
6) **Look for opportunities for self-discovery.** People often learn something about themselves and may find that they have grown in some respect as a result of their struggle with loss. Many people who have experienced tragedies and hardship have reported

better relationships, greater sense of strength even while feeling vulnerable, increased sense of self-worth, a more developed spirituality, and heightened appreciation for life.

7) **Nurture a positive view of yourself.** Developing confidence in your ability to solve problems and trusting your instincts helps build resilience.
8) **Keep things in perspective.** Even when facing very painful events, try to consider the stressful situation in a broader context and keep a long-term perspective. Avoid blowing the event out of proportion.
9) **Maintain a hopeful outlook.** An optimistic outlook enables you to expect that good things will happen in your life. Try visualizing what you want, rather than worrying about what you fear.
10) **Take care of yourself.** Pay attention to your own needs and feelings. Engage in activities that you enjoy and find relaxing. Exercise regularly. Taking care of yourself helps to keep your mind and body primed to deal with situations that require resilience.

- (American Psychological Association 2004)

Exercise Three

Ok, now comes the part where we are going to try to apply how people not just get through trauma, (using self statements, cognitive reappraisal, processing emotionally loaded areas), but may actually see themselves as having grown from the events. Not that it didn't make them suffer, but some how they've been changed. In some ways, if they look for it, for the better. Not that they or most of us wouldn't wish the traumatic event didn't happen. We wish it didn't. But since it did, is there any way it has moved your life in a direction where something positive might be said? You may find the trauma has shown you really do hold an inner strength, maybe it has helped you realize how important relationships are, perhaps your values have become strengthened, and maybe it has enhanced your spiritual life. Try to think about this: as hard as this has been, and clearly not something we would want anyone to endure, has there been something it gave you by having survived and come to this point?

My Trauma Description

What we'd like you to do at this point is to write or type a 2-3 page description of your traumatic event, with a much different focus. This time try to write it as if you can see how it has made a major, positive difference in your life. This may take some thought. Read the instructions a few times, and then think about where you are at this time in your life (literally and figuratively), and then write about the event looking back on it with this change already made inside of you. How it would feel, how your life might be different, how it would also be authentic, real. No one would ever ask for or wish for a trauma to occur to anyone, but when they do they sometimes change people in a positive way that might never have happened if the trauma hadn't occurred. Try to write in any way you can think of about how this difficult time has had a positive impact in your life.

Ok, again get some paper, and begin writing.

Read and re-read 3-4x/day for 7-10 days.

The following worksheet is provided to use in this exercise. Please feel free to review it, and use whatever suggestions you think would be useful to you.

Exercise 3 Worksheet

Change for the positive can also be helped by:

1) Being open to new possibilities.
2) Change in relationships. See if there is a chance to make it even better.
3) Increased sense of personal strength. If I got through this, I can get through a lot.
4) Greater appreciation of life in general. I should not take life for granted. It is mine to cherish.
5) Spiritual change & deepening of beliefs. Meaning is important, and we each can find this in our own spiritual path and search for values and meanings in our daily life.

Here are other suggestions that helped some people:

- Be realistically optimistic about life – hold beliefs that things can change for the better, and that you have the ability to help with that change.
- Set reasonable goals.
- Stressful events can be problems to be solved, and see what aspects of the situation are open to change.
- Find meaning and purpose in life's values and choices.
- Make a gift of your survival to others.
- Accept what is, and not what you think should be.
- Take actions where you can.
- Seek help and engage in kindness activities.
- Don't isolate yourself from others.
- Most lasting change comes only from times of adversity.
- Your thoughts can provoke emotion.
- Take it in manageable steps.
- You need some arousal to change.

- Try to see what these thoughts and situations are and see them as "triggers" to deal with.
- Reminders of the event should not be avoided, nor should safety behaviors and attempts to stop thoughts be encouraged.

What helps survivors grow?

1) Benefit seeking, finding and reminding - self: "No one deserves to go through what I did, but now I know I can get through this. I am a stronger person.", "I am wiser as a result of this.", "I am less afraid of change.", "I now savor daily pleasures."
2) Benefit seeking, finding and reminding – others: "This brought us all together.", "I think about others and how it could have been worse.", "I learned I am my brothers' keeper."
3) Engage in downward comparison: "I recognize that I need to accept help."
4) Establish a future orientation: "My view of what is important in life has changed.", "I see new possibilities and goals to work on.", "I am now able to focus on the fact that it happened and NOT on just how it happened.", "My view of what is important in life has changed."
5) Constructive meaning" "We (I) survived. We have a chance to live and I'm choosing life.", "I am no longer willing to be defined by my victimization.", "I survived for a purpose, I accept that responsibility. I owe it to.....to tell the story (honor their memory, share with others, prevent this from happening to others..).", "I moved from being a victim to a survivor to a thriver."
6) Be open to the support and help from others. Do not isolate yourself from those who care about you.

The three exercises and worksheets that are included to guide you through the three steps, will take some time. But the time is well spent, as it helps you look at the things that may have been hard to look at, and the exercises guide you through a way to reconstruct the way you remember and think about what happened, using steps drawn from strategies that have been helpful for other people who have suffered a significant trauma.

1) I walk down the street.
There is a deep hole in the sidewalk
I fall in.
I am lost...I am hopeless.
It isn't my fault.
It takes forever to find a way out.

2) I walk down the same street.
There is a deep hole in the sidewalk.
I pretend I don't see it.
I fall in again.
I can't believe I'm in the same place.
But it isn't my fault.
It still takes a long time to get out.

3) I walk down the same street.
There is a deep hole in the sidewalk
I see it is there.
I still fall in...it's a habit
My eyes are open
I know where I am
It is my fault.
I get out immediately.

4) I walk down the same street.
There is a deep hole in the sidewalk
I walk around it.

5) I walk down another street.

- Portia Nelson, *"Autobiography in Five Chapters"*

Personal Narrative Revisited

The following is another twist on the writing exercises. I offer it here as some people will prefer to write on their computers, and keep the information in secure files on their PCs or laptops. If you do, this may be another way to write your story, and to begin the process of making the changes you'd like.

With the use of computers, we have been able to try a variety of ways to manipulate the written word and how we perceive it. The following is an exercise I have used a bit in my practice, when someone is using a computer to write their exercises, and we have very simply utilized some of the power of word to change the way the words are presented.

Directions:

In this exercise we'd like you to think about a traumatic event or event that you're willing to work on. Take a moment and get the event or events clear in your mind. What we'd like you to then do is to describe the event in chronological order, from start to finish, as best as you can. In particular, we'd like you to describe the memories of the event, including sights, sounds, smells, as well as any thoughts or other parts that come to mind. Try not to write less than a page, or more than 3 pages in total, but be sure to include those images or memories that have contributed to your pain and difficulty in carrying them.

To help you see what we mean, we'd like you to look at an example. This is a common trauma, which may not be exactly comparable to yours. It's provided to show you in some detail what we are asking you to do.

Example:

It was a hot, rainy evening. I needed to go pick up some things at the store. I remember thinking something isn't right. This night doesn't feel right. I got in the car. It was sticky feeling. I adjusted the seat and mirrors, as someone else had last driven it. At the last minute, my wife Ann said she wanted to join me, and jumped in just as I was getting ready to pull out.

Traffic was light. I got the intersection right before the store where there is a 4 way stop. I stopped. Looked both ways, and pulled into the intersection. The next thing I remember was a BANG! Metal crushing, and feeling as if I was being dragged on and on forever! Then everything got quiet. I looked over to Ann. She wasn't moving. I yelled, Ann! Ann! Then I saw the blood. It was everywhere! All over her, the window, and the seat. I couldn't breathe. I thought I was going to pass out. I tried to move but couldn't. My legs were pinned under me. When I tried to loosen the seat-belt, my arm wouldn't move. The bone sticking out didn't look real. I remember thinking, "This is it. I'm going to die here because I needed bread for a sandwich". Oh, Ann she must be dead, I couldn't see her breathing! I should have seen it coming! It's my fault! And I can't even move to touch her!

It seemed like it took forever to get help. They told me later it was only a few minutes. Maybe I lost consciousness, or just couldn't face how bad it was. The funny thing is how little pain I felt physically. The EMT arrived, and I remember him asking me my name. At first, I couldn't speak, like I'd forgotten how! Then it all just came out. He was reassuring, and said he was going to check on my passenger. He asked her name, and I just started crying, and saying help her, but she's dead! I don't remember anything else until we were in the ambulance. It was so quiet. Then all the noise in the world, sirens, talking, radios seemed to be on all at once.

Then a new person, a woman said we were on our way to the hospital. Don't worry she said. Your wife is ok. She was just knocked out, and had a lot of cuts. She then said I had a broken bone in my arm, and they'll check me out further once I get to the emergency department. I had a few problems, but they could take care of them once we got to the hospital. This can't be real! It must be a dream. Please let me wake up!

Ok, there's the example. Now, we'd have you do a mindfulness exercise, similar to this;

So, once you've written your narrative. Just stop, and breathe. Try to pay attention to where you are, like you've done so many times in the past. Notice your in breath, and your out breath. Notice what it feels like to sit where you sit. Your feet on the floor. Where your arms are, notice any other feelings. Maybe tightness in some muscles, some heaviness. Don't try to do anything with those feelings other than to call them what they are. There may be thoughts you notice as well. Good. Use your mind to step back and see them for what they are, thoughts. Memories.

Then what I'd like you to do, when you do your writing is if your eyes were closed, to open them now, and pay attention to what's around you. Take in the room. The colors, shapes, smells. The sounds in the room. And outside of the room.

Now let's look back at what you wrote. If you're willing, then read it out loud to yourself. Then, what we'd like you do, is to go back and start to sort out the "facts" from the other parts of the memories. Using the example we just reviewed, it might look something like this. Highlight, "Just the Facts" (in this book the "highlight" is grey; you might want to use a yellow or different color highlighter when you do this).

It was a hot, rainy *evening. I needed to go pick up some things at the store. I remember thinking something isn't right. This night doesn't feel right. I got in the car. It was sticky feeling. I adjusted the seat and mirrors, as someone else had last driven it. At the last minute, my wife Ann said she wanted to join me, and jumped in just as I was getting ready to pull out.*

Traffic was light. I got to the intersection right before the store where there is a 4 way stop. I stopped. Looked both ways, and pulled into the intersection. The next thing I remember was a BANG! Metal crushing, and feeling as if I was being dragged on and on forever! Then everything got quiet. I looked over to Ann. She wasn't moving. I yelled, Ann! Ann! Then I saw the blood. It was everywhere! All over her, the window, and the seat. I couldn't breathe. I thought I was going to pass out. I tried to move but couldn't. My legs were pinned under me. When I tried to loosen the seatbelt, my arm wouldn't move. The bone sticking out didn't look real. I remember thinking, "This is it. I'm going to die here because I needed bread for a sandwich". Oh, Ann she must be dead, I couldn't see her breathing! I should have seen it coming! It's my fault! And I can't even move to touch her!

It seemed like it took forever to get help. They told me later it was only a few minutes. Maybe I lost consciousness, or just couldn't face how bad it was. The funny thing is how little pain I felt physically. The EMT arrived, and I remember him asking me my name. At first, I couldn't speak, like I'd forgotten how! Then it all just came out. He was reassuring, and said he was going to check on my passenger. He asked her name, and I just started crying, and saying help her, but she's dead! I don't remember anything else until we were in the ambulance. It was so quiet. Then all the noise in the world, sirens, talking, radios seemed to be on all at once.

Then a new person, a woman said we were on our way to the hospital. Don't worry she said. Your wife is ok. She was just knocked out, and had a lot of cuts. She then said I had a broken bone in my arm, and they'll check me out further once I get to the emergency department. I had a few problems, but they could take care of them once we got to the hospital. This can't be real! It must be a dream. Please let me wake up!

What did we just do? Remember the way minds work? They remember things, but they also add things. Judgments and evaluations? And they also present thoughts and feelings. We're not saying they aren't right or you shouldn't have them. Or, that you should argue with them, and try to change them into something more "real" or anything else. NO, what we are saying is to let this experience be what it is, a memory, a very powerful memory which brings along with it pain, and things that are difficult to bear. Rather than avoid those feelings and thoughts, you choose to go down this path, and NOT avoid those things that aren't avoidable, to face the thoughts and memories that are in fact a part of us, to see them as what they are.

There are thoughts, there are impressions, there are beliefs that in this example turned out not to be true such as the wife's death. We ask to see this memory as what it is. To respect it, and to respect what took place. And then to let it be seen as it is; nothing more or less. That's enough. That's everything.

In fact, if you look at this example now, we are going to take away everything that isn't a "fact". We might argue about what facts are or not, but again, if that's the case, please see what your mind is doing at that point. Let's see what this painful memory looks like, with those other parts gone or faded.

It was a hot, rainy evening. I needed to go pick up some things at the store. I remember thinking something isn't right. This night doesn't feel right. I got in the car. It was sticky feeling. I adjusted the seat and mirrors, as someone else had last driven it. At the last minute, my wife Ann said she wanted to join me, and jumped in just as I was getting ready to pull out.

Traffic was light. I got to the intersection right before the store where there is a 4 way stop. I stopped. Looked both ways, and pulled into the intersection. The next thing I remember was a BANG! Metal crushing, and feeling as if I was being dragged on and on forever! Then everything got quiet. I looked over to Ann. She wasn't moving. I yelled, Ann! Ann! Then I saw the blood. It was everywhere! All over her, the window, and the seat. I couldn't breathe. I thought I was going to pass out. I tried to move but couldn't. My legs were pinned under me. When I tried to loosen the seatbelt, my arm wouldn't move. The bone sticking out didn't look real. I remember thinking, "This is it. I'm going to die here because I needed bread for a sandwich". Oh, Ann she must be dead, I couldn't see her breathing! I should have seen it coming! It's my fault! And I can't even move to touch her!

It seemed like it took forever to get help. They told me later it was only a few minutes. Maybe I lost consciousness, or just couldn't face how bad it was. The funny thing is how little pain I felt physically. The EMT arrived, and I remember him asking me my name. At first, I couldn't speak, like I'd forgotten how! Then it all just came out. He was reassuring, and said he was going to check on my passenger. He asked her name, and I just started crying, and saying help her, but she's dead! I don't remember anything else until we were in the ambulance. It was so quiet. Then all the noise in the world, sirens, talking, radios seemed to be on all at once.

Then a new person, a woman said we were on our way to the hospital. Don't worry she said. Your wife is ok. She was just knocked out, and had a lot of cuts. She then said I had a broken bone in my arm, and they'll check me out further once I get to the emergency department. I had a few problems, but they could take care of them once we got to the hospital. This can't be real! It must be a dream. Please let me wake up!

We'd like you to look back on your written description. If you find you're unable or it's too difficult to fade the letters you might be able to highlight them or cross them out (the strike key is great for this). Even if you just look at them with the perspective of in this moment, looking at what is going on, you will gain some space with those very painful past events that have been so heavy and hard to have. Try completing the exercise this way, by HIGHLIGHTING THE FACTS (some may quibble about them, but do the best you can), and then STRIKE OUT the impressions, memories that may or may not be true, judgments, distortions and words that are anything but incontrovertible facts. See how you feel as you read just the facts.

There are two kinds of suffering: the suffering that leads to more suffering and the suffering that leads to the end of suffering. If you are not willing to face the second kind of suffering, you will surely continue to experience the first.

- Ajahn Chah, from "A Still Forest Pool"

Chapter Twelve

No Man is an Island *(You've got to have Friends)* *The Importance of Social Relations*

Janice

Janice from the time of her loss was in near constant contact with someone, either family or friends. When her son died in the bus accident, and her daughter had suffered a head injury, her world became hell. Time lost meaning, and even now she couldn't believe it'd been 9 months. But the clouds were lifting. And as they did there were her parents. They'd always been close, but now they were there without even being asked. Her other daughter was never forgotten. Her husband had also been destroyed by the loss. But his family had also pitched in, and between the visits and the phone calls she knew they were there. Friends also stayed with her. Even though she had begged them to go away, to just leave her to suffer, they didn't go that far. They were always respectful, but there was no doubt she was on their minds and in their hearts. Food arrived at just the right time, and the lawn got mowed. Work friends were also amazing. Her job was hers when she was ready. The pain was great, but there was a way through this. Maybe.

One of the most consistent findings in the psychological literature about who does well and who doesn't following a traumatic event is the powerful role that friends and family can play in getting through hard times and tragic events. If we needed to pick just one factor to stack the deck for a good recovery, pick social relationships.

The spouse, family and friends play critical roles to support and help the person who suffered a trauma in his or her healing process.

This makes a lot of sense. The symptoms of PTSD, include feeling cut off from others, social withdrawal, and having a loss of positive feelings toward things that used to be important to us, as well as feelings of isolation and feeling removed from our social connections. If one has a family that doesn't give in to your efforts to push them away, and instead they stick around and still help and give support to you at those times of need, that's a very powerful force for the future.

In our treatment of survivors of motor vehicle crashes, we tried as often as we could to include the significant other of the survivor. The significant other of the survivor of the trauma just wanted to learn what had really happened to change their loved one so much. The partner needed to understand what PTSD was, and what they could expect as a result to their loved one struggling with it. They needed to understand the treatment, what was the need for exposure, and why the survivor was going off and doing these strange exercises to try to relax. And perhaps most importantly, what could they do to help. The social support was real, and ever present.

This factor, the role that social support can play, has been found to be crucial for our returning veterans, rape survivors, and for the survivors dealing with the other losses and tragedies that affect our lives. On a related topic, social support is offered in the metaphor from *The Snowball*, the biography of Warren Buffet.

Buffet tells the story of when he was 16; he had 2 things on his mind, cars and girls. As he states he wasn't very good with girls, he thought about cars, as he had more luck with cars. He then raises the question of what if at 16 a genie had appeared, and said Warren I'm going to give you the car of your choice. It will be here tomorrow, and it will be all yours. Having heard genie stories he asks, "What's the catch?" The genie answers, "The catch is this is going to be the last car you will ever get in your life. So the car has got to last a lifetime". If that had happened, and he picked the car, can you imagine knowing it would have to last a lifetime what he or anyone would do? What would you do? He'd read the manual numerous times, he'd always keep it garaged, if there was a little dent or scratch he would get it fixed right away. He would baby that car, as it had to last a lifetime. Buffet then makes the argument that is exactly the position you are given with your body and mind. You only get one, its got to last a lifetime. It's easy to ride them for many years, but if you don't take care of it, the body becomes a wreck in 40 yrs., just like a car would. He concludes, what you do today determines how your mind and body will operate 10, 20, 30 years from now.

Now I would further the metaphor, to relationships, just imagine the same scenario. You are given the gift of a partner, someone to cherish and love, but the relationship must last a lifetime, you won't be given the chance to get another. What if you thought of the relationship in the same way? If you did, then every word, every gesture would matter to you. It would be important because if you didn't pay attention and value it, the same erosion and destruction would occur. And if there is a wreck, something goes wrong in the relationship, you would try to restore that relationship as well as you could; it would be critical to you to do so, as you would fully be aware of what losing it would mean. To keep that type of awareness requires mindfulness, and an awareness of the importance of how every word and action, has a consequence, and they add up. Good maintenance can go a long way to having a wonderful relationship, just like with a car, if we give it the proper care.

Could our minds and our hearts be big enough just to hang out in that space where we're not entirely certain about who's right and who's wrong? Could we have no agenda when we walk into a room with another person, not know what to say, not make this person right or wrong? Could we see, hear, feel other people as they really are? It is powerful to practice this way, because we'll find ourselves continually rushing around to try to feel secure again– to make ourselves or them right or wrong. But true communication can happen only in that open space.

- Pema Chodron

What should you do if there are no close relationships?

For some people, the tragic events that occur can occur at a time when there are no truly close friends. No spouse, or family or even friends who are there in their moment of need. What then? I consider myself very fortunate that I had the support that was there in my moment of need. But I have had the chance to know a good number of people who are hurt, and suffering at a time when they feel very much alone, and in fact, some are cut off from the typical supports we would hope are found in most people's lives.

Social support at these moments, may come from other sources. Perhaps there are support groups, some in mental health, community or church settings. AA for many is a place where the support that is offered without judgment or cost, and is lifesaving. Some people will find volunteering an invaluable place to connect and find support. Often it is by giving to others in our time of need, that we are helped in finding our own way. There is a truly positive experience that can occur when we give of ourselves to others.

In each of these settings is an opportunity to find new friends. People who share our interests, backgrounds, or desires to join in some experience can be a great source of support.

Think back in your own experiences if there are places, or ways that social support can be found. While again, not easy for many people, experience and research support the very real benefit that can come from the connection with other people.

Social Support Assessment

Social support can show up in lots of different ways: sometimes we are looking for companionship, other times for someone to help us when we are need. Read the following questions, and ask yourself if in general you think you look for social support if it were available to you, a little of the time, some of the time, or most of the time.

Is there someone to help if you:

Are bed ridden?
Need someone to talk to?
Need to be driven to an appointment?
Show you love and caring?
Confide in?
Give you advice?
Share your private worries or fears with?
Enjoy your life with?
Make you feel as if you are wanted or needed?

Hopefully, you'll answer the questions in ways that show you have strong social support. If not, then ask yourself if there might be ways to improve the relationships in your life.

Things to Do Now

What can a friend or family member do to support someone following a trauma? It's hard to know what to say, and they are often difficult to get close to. In fact, sometimes we even find ourselves angry at our loved one for not getting better, and for leaving us emotionally so alone. I miss him (her). Sometimes survivors will have similar feelings about themselves.

It is hard to know what to do, but the road back is certainly better traveled with someone by your side.

Some practical things that may make sense include:

1. Taking them to doctor appointments or other appointments. They may be hurt or on medication, or emotionally vulnerable. Someone to drive can be a big help.
2. Provide emotional support. Talk if they want, or at least offer.
3. Show physical support. Give a hug, a rub, reach out to touch them. A physical touch can be powerful when you feel cut off from others.
4. Make sure to include them in things that might give them joy.
5. Share your life with them, even if they appear to be indifferent or not caring. If that person cared before, they are still in there. That role is important to them, even if unreachable for a while.
6. Shop for food and run other errands (unless this is a type of avoidance). If possible include them in these activities.

7. Invite over important friends and family, even if this is hard. This is a unique time. No one can do it alone, and any help that leads someone out of a dark place is a good thing.
8. Treat them how you would like to be treated. This is a person you are probably the closest to in the whole world. If you don't reach out for them, then who will?
9. Be patient. Some things take time. Healing doesn't just happen, even if you're given the right medicine.

"Too often we underestimate the power of a touch, a smile, a kind word, a listening ear, an honest compliment, or the smallest act of caring, all of which have the potential to turn life around"

- Leo Buscaglia

In my own case, the support I had in the hospital was critical. While people had to live their own lives, someone kept popping in just to check on things. Most importantly, I knew my wife had support. She had people with her, and that helped me worry less about her, and gave me more energy (what little I had) to focus on what I needed to be doing each moment of the day. Rehabilitation was long, and painful. I was lucky I had a friend and colleague who was my occupational therapist and hand therapist. She allowed me to have the needed confidence in her so I could just focus on my exercises, and deal with getting to and from her clinic. Friends kept stopping in too. They brought games and magazines, most of which I never played or read. But their coming gave me so much. That was the medicine I needed. Family, however, was the most important. My wife was amazing. I never realized, because we had never had to deal with such an event, that she could do so much. I have two sons, who also grew in ways that, while uncomfortable at first (who wants your son helping you get around), I think in the end made us all better people. As a psychologist, largely in private practice, I have worked alone in my office most of the time, so my circle of friends is small and close. They were there, including some surprises such as friends' husbands who I never really thought I was that close to, but suddenly they were there to drive me to work when I couldn't drive (just talk), and gave me so much support, all without my asking, or ever expecting it. All I really know is, I was lucky to have so many people around.

Bette Midler – "Friends"

And I am all alone
There is no one here beside me
And my problems have all gone
There is no one to deride me

But you got to have friends
The feeling's oh so strong
You got to have friends
To make that day last long
*I had some **friends** but their gone*
Someone came and took them away
And from the dusk till the dawn
Here is where I'll stay

*Standing at the end of **the road**, boys*
Waiting for my new friends to come
I don't care if I'm hungry or bored
I'm gonna get me some of them

Cause you got to have friends
La la la la la la la la la
Friends, I said you,
Oh you, yeah you, I said
You got to have some Friends
Something about friends
Just right friends
Friends, friends, friends
I had some friends oh but they're all gone, gone
Someone came and snatched them away
And from the dusk until the very dawn
You know here is where I gotta stay
Here is where I gotta stay
And I'm standing at the end of a real long road
*And I'm waiting for my **new friends** to come*
I don't care if I'm hungry or freezing cold
I'm gonna get me some of them

Cause you got to have friends
That's right friends
Friends,….I gotta see my, I gotta see my
I gotta see all of my friends, friends
Friends, friends, friends

CHAPTER THIRTEEN

Kindness, Forgiveness and Meaning

Marsha

Marsha kept thinking about how she'd been so weak, at just the time her family needed her. The death of her son in Afghanistan was just so overwhelming. She was lost. Adrift. Her husband tried at first, but after awhile he stopped asking about how he could help, and just seemed to give up too. And her other son Jacob tried, but he was spending so much time around the house that she ended up just screaming at him again and again until finally he too stopped being there. She'd hurt them so much by her actions. She didn't know why she'd been so mean, but the hurt and anger was just in every part of her being. But, over time things did get better. Her husband and she were doing better, and Jacob had started joining them for dinner on Sundays. They'd forgiven her. Now if she could just forgive herself. Every time she got a little closer to forgiveness, then the image of her son getting blown up returned, and she just felt so angry at those who did that, and those who sent him there. Would that ever leave?

One area that we are learning about is the importance of coming to peace with oneself and those strong feelings that swell up and seem to block our recovery. Compassion and kindness are two building blocks that can help transform one's worries and anxieties into something that can be carried and lived with. To do this, one needs to learn to cultivate the loving kindness like a mother toward a newborn child or family member.

People who suffer PTSD and other anxiety disorders can often be extremely hard on themselves. They are frequently frustrated by how limited their lives have become, and blame themselves for not being able to get past these barriers. The blame can take the form of not being strong enough (as they compare themselves to others), or yelling at themselves for having "something wrong with their head" (when maybe they are doing the best they can, or anyone could do), and hating their panic attacks and bouts of anger. PTSD can cause a daily struggle for people following trauma. They may be angry at the person who did this to them, at themselves for things they failed to do, and feel ashamed they can't pull themselves out of this and get on with their lives as they think they should.

The first question again is how is the way you are feeling or acting helping or not helping lead you to the life you'd like to have? If those feelings and thoughts about you are not helping, and how could they, then perhaps it is time to try something else. Even more important, as the focus of this book is about, the people who learn to be more kind and more compassionate, tend to do a lot better and get over their PTSD faster than those who don't learn these skills. But to be kind to oneself is not always a natural or easy thing to do.

Let's offer a few ways to start. First, compassion and kindness are not feelings. They're actions. That's important because as we've learned we can't always (or ever) control our feelings, but we do have a lot to say about our actions. What we say, what we do with our hands (make a fist or shake a hand), or where we move our feet (what actions will you do?) are determined by you. These are choices we all have. Compassion is shown by the way we treat others. Kindnesses are acts that we know when granted. You can control these even at times when you don't always feel so compassionate or kind. This is once again something you can do something about right now. You don't need to wait for a better moment or for your feelings to be exactly in line so you can "act" with compassion or kindness, toward others, or towards yourself.

These actions then give you a direction. They give you a better direction if you have a good idea of what you want to move toward. What are the important things in your life that have led you to try to get past the pain of your trauma? Are there reasons in your life that have made this journey worthwhile? Maybe they involve your relationships, with your wife and children; maybe with your family. Maybe you want to do more with your life in terms of your work, or your education. Perhaps you want to rejoin your life with friends, with your community. Maybe you just want to take better care of yourself, body, mind and soul. Whatever it is, the more in touch you are with the reasons you want to change, the better your commitment to doing so.

Being angry with oneself, or holding onto the anger towards the one who harmed you, can often get in the way of those goals of living the life you would like to have. This is why compassion and kindness are part of finding a better balance and peace within oneself. The only one who can let you off the anger hook is you. Part of letting yourself off, is making the choice you want that, and a willingness then to do what that decision requires. "Who is your anger hurting?" is an important question. You? Your loved ones? Does it even have an effect on the one you are most angry at?

Rise up through forgiveness. Perhaps nothing so weighs the spirit as the sadness engendered by broken relationships. Forgiveness believes in the human capacity to change. It offers each of us the possibility of reclaiming higher ground by giving another human being the chance to become someone new. While one of the most precious gifts we can offer another, the effect it has on us is equally dramatic: suddenly our world feels different, unhindered by our need to keep the other in lockup.

- The Monks of New Skete

I will share two exercises drawn from the Acceptance and Commitment approach you heard earlier that might help you get started.

When old wounds, painful images and feelings come up, the first instinct in many of us is to push them away and to avoid them as best as we can. If you notice yourself doing that, please stop. This is the opportunity you're looking for.

Why? Remember if you do what you always did, you can only expect the same result. In this case, rather than pushing the pain away, instead make room for it, welcome it in if you would, for the chance of something new happening. If you only push your pain away, there isn't time to help it heal. We'll return to the physical analogy we used earlier in the book; if you had a problem with your back, or your teeth, you might try to push it away for awhile, but sooner or later the time would come to go to a doctor, or a dentist, and get the best care you could if you wanted to get better. The same approach is suggested for your emotional wounds: the fears, the anger, the panic, the shame and all the blame you inflict upon yourself.

THE GUEST HOUSE

This being human is a guest house.
Every morning a new arrival.

A joy, a depression, a meanness,
some momentary awareness comes
As an unexpected visitor.

Welcome and entertain them all!

Even if they're a crowd of sorrows,
who violently sweep your house
empty of its furniture,
still treat each guest honorably.
He may be clearing you out
for some new delight.

The dark thought, the shame, the malice,
meet them at the door laughing,
and invite them in.

Be grateful for whoever comes,
because each has been sent
as a guide from beyond.

- Jelaluddin Rumi, translation by Coleman Barks

To break the cycle of anxiety and the avoidance of things that have constricted and limited your life, you need to practice being kind to yourself, and stop buying into all that stuff that your mind came up with about you and your emotional pain (remember - thoughts are just thoughts, feelings just feelings; nothing more, nothing less).

Let's try an exercise to see how this might work for you:

One way to learn about kindness and compassion is to do the opposite of what you might want to do (starting to sound familiar yet?), but this time in the service of others, and as a way to join them and not feel so isolated. To breathe in and invite in what feels bad, while giving away what feels good and joyful. Breathing in pain and breathing out pain is a very old meditative technique known as Tonglen ("meaning giving and receiving"). The notion of welcoming in pain and giving away good may seem weird, or opposite to what at first makes sense. This is exactly why it is a powerful approach. Remember, almost all of our battles begin within, so must our healing.

When you embrace what you don't like, you "*transform it*". That type of transformation will release you from those things that had held you, from seeking only pleasure, avoiding things you don't like, releasing you from fear and self absorption, allowing you to grow your capacity for love and compassion.

Let's try this exercise.

Tonglen Meditation

Find a comfortable place to sit where you won't be disturbed. Find a comfortable position either sitting or lying down.

Gently close your eyes and begin to focus on the rhythm of your breathing. Breathing in and breathing out. Then begin to bring your mind to something painful or hurtful. This might be a recent event, a period when you felt anxious or upset, or perhaps the trauma that you are struggling with right now. With your next breath in, visualize taking in all of that negativity and pain associated with the memory. Breathe in the discomfort with the thought in your mind that this feeling that you're having is also being felt by people all over the world. You are not alone in this feeling. These feelings of pain, suffering and anxiety have been felt by numerous people throughout history up until this present moment.

The hope for yourself and for the others that you imagine is that everyone will be free of this suffering, this struggle, blame or shame that can follow the trauma you experienced and the pain that came with it. With that thought in your mind on each exhalation try to imagine breathing out relief, joy and good will. Do the breathing slowly with full awareness of the rising and falling of your chest. Try to be aware of and connected with your pain as you breathe in and as you breathe out wish for others to find relief from the suffering that they have in their own life experiences and hurt. If you find that breathing in anxiety and uncomfortable feelings gets too heavy or feels too uncomfortable try to imagine breathing in to a large space, or even better, that your own heart is a large, even infinite space. Imagine that you are breathing in to your heart, having it grow more and more with every out breath, until there is enough space within your heart for all the worries, pain and uncomfortable feelings. And then with each out breath imagine that you open up your entire self, so that you no longer need to avoid or push away worries, anxieties or other uncomfortable feelings, as you are now open to whatever arises inside of you.

If your mind wanders, or you find yourself feeling distracted just be aware of that and return your attention back to your effort of welcoming in your pain and suffering and then releasing kindness and compassion for everyone who suffers. Continue this course of giving and then receiving for as long as you care or desire.

And then when you are ready, slowly begin to place your awareness on other thoughts and feelings and what's going on around you, slowly opening your eyes with the hope of bringing this new kind of observing your experiences throughout the day and your life.

- As adapted from the work of Pema Chodron

Self compassion has been associated with improvement in those who suffer with symptoms of PTSD. What do we mean by self compassion? Imagine the compassion you might give to someone who you see suffering. They may have had something bad occur, and you are pulled to them to try to comfort them in that time of hurt. Your first impulse might be to offer them an arm to support them, to put a blanket around them, to offer a few words of encouragement. You wouldn't be yelling at them for what happened. You demonstrate a kindness that has tremendous power at just those times when we are so vulnerable and helpless. Now image that person is you. You don't berate or judge immediately. You instead offer yourself the same kindness. You see life as full of difficulties, and we all have flaws.

An exercise, which I have started using lately shows how to get to these feelings of compassion in perhaps a more natural way, to form a bridge to these feelings.

Building Self Compassion

Close your eyes and get comfortable. As you settle back, focus on your breathing; simple…in and out. Find a rhythm that is comfortable and natural for you. Be aware of how it feels to just sit where you are sitting. And with this awareness of you, I'd like you to imagine the following scene: Create an image of someone who has experienced a trauma like the one you are struggling with. Imagine, as best as you can, what it is that person might be going through. Their thoughts, their feelings, all the things that go on inside of them. Think of how the experience may have impacted their life. Try to take a moment to fully realize what it would mean for someone like that. Then imagine that person was a friend, or a friend of a friend, perhaps even a family member, a brother, a sister, or a daughter or son. Now, with that image fully in your mind, imagine what words, what gestures, what your reaction would be, or what you would like it to be that would be most helpful for that person.

Would you be as harsh on them as you may have been on yourself? Would you begin with what they should have done, or how they need to judge the events? To be critical?

Or, would you treat them as they need to be treated, how they deserve to be treated? With understanding and compassion. Not judging, not telling them what they should have done, or felt, or anything else. Take a moment to see instead what you would give...... and how they might react, and be helped by that gift.

Then, take a moment, and allow that image to shift over to yourself... and see yourself acting like that towards yourself, if only for a moment...and how that might feel. Then, when you're ready, I'd like you to once again shift your attention back to the place where you are, to where you're sitting, and what it feels like to be where you are... being aware of yourself, the feelings, thoughts, sensations inside of you.... and aware of the sounds, and the sensations outside of you. And when you're ready slowly open your eyes, aware, and present here. Now. Taking a moment or two, to let whatever feelings arose settle and take those with you in a positive fashion to heal and to grow.

If you would like an audio version of this exercise a downloadable version can be found at www.transformingtragedy.com.

To be human means we are not perfect. Drawing on a biblical example, even Jesus, who is the Son of God, when in the desert had his moments of doubt, to feel he too was forsaken. Certainly one of the lessons there is that when even Jesus is in a human form, he experiences what it is to be human. To have doubts, fears and to feel abandoned. It must be a part of the human condition. Self-compassion is where we can bring this same understanding of what it means to be human, to express kindness towards ourselves for not being perfect, and to accept those flaws as natural, and a part of all of us. Including you and me. Self-compassion shows up in how we can be more tolerant of ourselves, to put that same blanket of kindness round ourselves rather than being harsh and cruel for what we imagine we should have done or been capable of. We try to maintain a balance about who we are, and not see ourselves as seriously worse than others, or lacking in some important way.

One of the leaders in this area is a dynamic psychologist at the University of Texas, Austin, Kristin Neff. She has developed a scale that measures our self-compassion. If you are interested you can find the scale at (www.self-compassion.org) along with a way to score and understand how your self compassion would look based upon her scale. Interested readers can also find more on this in her excellent book on self compassion, listed in the appendix.

Forgiveness

Learning to forgive is hard. People who have learned to forgive have been found to improve their health, report less hurt, stress, anger, depression, and illness while having more energy, hope, optimism, compassion and love. But, many people hear the word forgiveness and think it means they are weak, or condoning the past, or forgetting past wrongs, ignoring hurt and pain. None of this is true. When Pope John Paul II met to forgive his assassin he wasn't condoning the act, instead he was extending mercy and compassion. Forgiveness is one of the most courageous and powerful acts you can do for yourself. It's about letting go. It's a gift to yourself. Who is punished by your lack of forgiveness? It means letting go of being a victim. The price of holding onto a victim's anger, shame, regret and pain is great.

Only you, and you alone can do this. Not embracing forgiveness stacks the deck that you will stay stuck with the feelings that hurt you, not just the one who actually hurt you. We can't guarantee that this exercise will work. I can assure you that the step in this direction is huge, and it opens the door to a multitude of changes in the positive direction.

Letting Go of the Anchor of Anger

Let's begin by just first getting settled in a place where you can be fairly still and undisturbed by outside noise or intrusions. Once there, try to get comfortable and focus first on your breathing, like you've learned in so many of these exercises. Just paying attention to the rising and falling of your breath. It is always there to help focus you if you drift too much at anytime or just want to let that be place to settle.

Then, let your mind go back to that place you just can't seem to let go of. That past event where you were hurt. Allow that memory to come, in all its details, including the feelings that are there; anger perhaps, shame, resentment, and perhaps even a sense of how wrong it was and how much injustice occurred. Think as fully as you can about the event. Mull it over. Let all the feelings, the details, the images, come along with the memories of the details. Remember as you can, what happened. Who was there? Besides you was there anyone else? Did others get hurt as well? What was the hurt? What didn't happen then that your mind tells you should have happened or how someone, maybe you, maybe others might have done something to change the event. Let all feelings to come in. Pain, confusion, helplessness? Where is that pain now? How do you experience it? If you feel it physically, where? How large, how deep? Don't avoid any part of it. Not now.

Then, with the mindfulness you've learned, step back a bit and see how your mind, your thoughts your beliefs, and your feelings get tied to it. Anchored with it. There probably is a judgment there. If there is see it as that. Blame, injustice, a wrong. Again, with that space your mind can give you see it as it is. Thoughts as thoughts, feelings as feelings, judgments as judgments.

Then to distance it even more, see the memory tied from then to now with an anchor stuck in the event, and a long line or chain hooking it from the past to your present moment. And with that distance watch it play out as it happened again, this time in your mind as if it were a movie or play and you are in the here and now watching it. See the person doing the hurt. See who is to blame for that. And there you are in the scene as you watch it from this perspective.

And then, following the chain, those links to the past memory back to yourself here and now, and ask yourself who is responsible for letting go of that feeling? Who has a say in that? Who carries that hurt, that anger, that sense of wrong. No one argues it is right or wrong. That it is true or untrue. Just, the question, who can let it go? That person who did the hurt back then? The one the chain is anchored to? You know the answer. There is only person who holds that power.

Or, does the memory, as it is anchored with that heavy weight and chain tie you so powerfully, that you are not in control of you, but this feeling is in fact in charge of you. And, with that image in mind, just imagine if you stopped the struggle. You've faced the hurt, and you realize that each time you let the memory in, it has pulled you back to that place. The place of hurt and pain, anger and resentment.

If you were willing, to cut that chain, and with it to let go of all that pain, range and anger, what would that show? Does it mean anything less if that hurt is not felt so powerfully? Or is there a victory if you could let it go, and take charge of your life, and all the energy, and power that had been anchored to that intense feeling. The anger less and less, until one day the forgiveness takes hold, who achieves what they want? You do. Free of the hurt. Instead of continuing to be dragged back by that anchor of pain, cut the chain, feel the freedom, and think of what you would do then? See that as if it were to happen right now. See the chain break, or be cut, and fall apart, letting the past go back to where it belongs, leaving the present where it belongs, not blocked by that. What then?

How would you like you to live your life, if this was no longer in the way it has to be, to carry that pain so long? When this is put in its place, it does not mean that the wrong is gone, it means simply that the forgiveness is done for you. Forgiveness is something only you can give. And the one who gains the most is you, as you free yourself from the weight of having to drag all that pain and suffering along each time the memory arrives. So you can live more and more the way you'd like to. There is much truth in the idea that "the best revenge is living well". But what if the idea of revenge didn't even need to be there? Just you and the desire to move in the direction you would like. Imagine that as fully as you can.....Imagine how that life could be, if even for a moment. Then, when you are ready, come back fully aware of this moment, and how this has already started.

Meaning

People want things to make sense. When tragedy happens, we have a need to understand what happened and why. Kushner raises the question that perhaps things happen for no reason, that there is randomness in the universe. Then while people look for connections striving to make sense of things including their ideas of God that sometimes things just happen.

"A big burly samurai comes to the wise man and says, "Tell me the nature of heaven and hell" and the roshi looks

at him in the face and says, "Why should I tell a scruffy, disgusting, miserable slob like you?" the samurai starts to get purple in the face, his hair starts to stand up, but the roshi won't stop, he keeps saying, "a miserable worm like you, do you think I should tell you anything?" consumed by rage, the samurai draws his sword, and he is just about to cut the head off the roshi. Then the roshi says, "That's hell", the samurai, who in fact is a sensitive person, instantly gets it that he has created his own hell, he was deep in hell. It was black and hot, filled with hatred, self-protection, anger, and resentment, so much he was going to kill this man. Tears filled his eyes and he starts to cry and he puts his palms together and the roshi says, "That's heaven."

- Pema Chodron

One way to look at these experiences is that there isn't any heaven or hell except how we relate to our world.

It is important that this process of searching takes place. Victor Frankl, perhaps one of the world's leading experts in psychiatry, in his book, "Man's Search for Meaning", describes how even his survival of the Nazi concentration camp can't be meaningless. He finds that how he carries the memory becomes a vital part of the experience.

Trauma, and life's tragedies force us to very uncomfortable places. Our ideas of the world are shattered. Nothing makes sense. People often offer words trying to give that meaning, but the words can't be received or accepted.

Harold Kushner in his book "When Bad Things Happen to Good People" addresses this by citing scripture. Kushner relates the story of Exodus with Moses when he came down from Mt. Sinai, and saw the Israelites worshipping the golden calf. He threw down the tablets of the Ten Commandments and they shattered. There is a Jewish legend that tells us that while Moses was climbing down the mountain with the two stone tablets where he had written the Ten Commandments he had no trouble carrying them although they were very large, heavy slabs of stone and the path was steep. While they were extremely heavy, they had been described by God, inscribed by God and, therefore, were precious to him and easy for him to bear. But when Moses came upon the people dancing around the golden calf the legend goes that the words disappeared from the stone. They were just blank stones again and now they were too heavy for him to hold on to. Kushner explains that we can bear any burden if we thought there was a meaning to what we were doing.

In a related way, you make it harder for someone to accept their illness and their misfortunes or family tragedies, if you tell them it has no meaning. Parents are able to carry the burden much better when they see it as part of a plan, even if its one they can't comprehend. If the illness or trauma however is meaningless, and just cruel, it becomes impossible to bear. Kushner suggests that the bad things that happen to us in this world do not have meaning when they happen to us. They do not happen for any good reason that would cause us to accept them willingly. But we give them that the meaning. We can redeem the tragedies from senselessness by imposing meaning in them. The question we should be asking is not why did this happen to me and why did I deserve this, which is unanswerable and pointless. The better question now that this has happened to me, what am I going to do about it?

Kushner discusses Harriet Schiff's book the *Brave Parent*, which recalls how a clergyman took her aside and said, "that while this is a painful time for you, I know you will get through it because God never sends us more of a burden than we can bear. He let this happen to you because he knows that you are strong enough to handle it." She remembers her reaction was that "if only I was a weaker person my son would be alive."

Kushner raises the explanation that God sends us the burden not because we are strong enough to handle it; that is wrong. Faith in God sends us the problem. When we try to deal with it we find that we are not strong, we are weak, we get tired, we get angry, overwhelmed. We begin to wonder how we will ever make it through the years. When we reach the limits of our own strength and courage, something unexpected happens. We find the encouragement coming from a source outside ourselves and then with the knowledge that we are not alone, that God is by our side, we manage to go on.

Tragic events often force us to confront our mortality. This is often one of the most basic things that we try desperately to forget. Escaping death strips away the shroud that covered the illusion that somehow either death will elude us, or death is a very long way away.

Gilgamesh, the original seeker and tragic figure, was seeking the secret of eternal life from Utnapishtim. His journey ends with the knowledge that immortality is not for man, instead "The life which shall seek us thou will not find: for when the Gods created mankind, they allotted death to mankind... (therefore) let thy belly be full: day and night be thy merry: make every day be a day of rejoicing... this is the lot of mankind".

According to an ancient Sufi story, a king who lived in the Middle Eastern land is torn between happiness and despondency. The time came when the king finally got tired of himself and his despondency, and wants to seek a way out. He became hopeless and suicidal. He went to a wise man and said "I want to be like you. Can you give me something that will bring balance, serenity and wisdom into my life? I will pay any price you ask." The wise man said I may be able to help you, but the price is so great that your entire kingdom would not be sufficient payment for it therefore it will be a gift to you, if you will honor it. The king gave his assurances and the wise man left. A few weeks later he returned and handed the king an ornate box carved in jade. The king opened the box and found a simple gold ring inside. Some letters were inscribed on the ring. The inscription read, "This too will pass." What is the meaning of this said the king? The Wiseman said, "Wear this ring always. Whatever happens before you call it good or bad, touch this ring and read the inscription. That way you will always be at peace". "This too will pass". What is it about those simple words that make it so powerful? This simple truth we all too often forget.

- As retold from a recounting of this story by Eckhart Tolle

Dr. Viktor Frankl discusses how life is not a quest for pleasure, but rather a quest for meaning; that the greatest task any person has is to find the meaning in his or her life. Suffering in and of itself is meaningless. We give our suffering meaning by the way in which we respond to it. Frankl offers the advice that when we are facing the challenge of one's death, it is imperative to live as if you're living for the second time and had acted as wrong the first time as you are about to act now. It is the opportunity to act properly on the potentialities of our actions, to fulfill meaning that is affected by the irreversibility of our lives. Frankl shares his belief in reconciliation with revenge and remarked "I do not forget any good deed done to me, and I do not carry a grudge for a bad one." He carried that idea and remarked that even a vile Nazi criminal, a seemingly hopeless madman, has potential to transcend evil or insanity by making responsible choices.

"If we really understood and remembered that life was impermanent, we would do everything we could to make the other person happy right here and right now. If we spend twenty-four hours being angry at our beloved, it is because we are ignorant of impermanence."

- Thich Nhat Hanh

Thus shall you think of all this fleeting world:
A star at dawn, a bubble in a stream;
A flash of lightning in a summer cloud,
A flickering lamp, a phantom, and a dream.

- from the "Diamond Sutra"

CHAPTER FOURTEEN

Random Thoughts

Usually we define our enemy as a person, an external agent, whom we believe is causing harm to us or to someone we hold dear. But such an enemy is dependent on many conditions and is impermanent. One moment, the person may act as an enemy; at yet another moment, he or she may become your best friend. This is a truth that we often experience in our own lives. But negative thoughts and emotions, the inner enemy, will always remain the enemy. They are your enemy today, they have been your enemy in the past, and they will remain your enemy in the future as long as they reside within your mind.

- the Dalai Lama

"The voyage of discovery lies not in finding new landscapes, but in having new eyes."

- Marcel Proust

I come to this point with a few things that are important for me to share, but as I thought about them, they didn't quite fit neatly into any of the chapters.

My Difficult Gift Box

One is a story that came to me from a friend, Dr. Cris Blanchard, a very gifted therapist, who worked largely with cancer survivors. The nature of leading a cancer survivor group is that one often needs to confront those things that you would chose not to face. The mood can get very dark very quickly, and it is often up to the therapist to try to help the group understand and deal with those feelings. One evening the group was grappling with a number of hard issues, the deaths of two group members, a worsening of the condition for another, and changes for the worse in the remaining members. Cris shared how the group just became paralyzed. While generally extremely capable to find some way to help the group process and find some meaning in the session, she too was stuck in the powerful emotion and thoughts that are no different for therapists than group members. It was very quiet. And heavy. She remembers thinking there ought to be something she should or could do here, but it didn't come to her. After what seemed like an interminable period of time, one of the group members spoke up. What she said went something like this. "I remember a thing my pastor told me that might help the group. I know it helps me when I most need it. When I get overwhelmed, with the disease, the treatments, the losses, the things that seem too hard to bear, I stop and think of my cancer as a gift. A very difficult gift that came in a box, all wrapped up with everything that comes with it. I can't give the gift back, but need to see it for all that it contains. It certainly contains some awful things. Pain, worry, and despair. But also in the box are other things that were given along with it; appreciation for life, not taking my family for granted, not even for one day. And to see the pain, the pain we're feeling right now as a gift too. I might not want it, but it is part of being fully human. I miss the women who died, and feel bad for all of us that are struggling. But this just helps me realize all the more how much life is worth holding onto, and how precious all these feelings and moments are. I wouldn't wish this illness on anyone, but it has given me a lot. I might have gone through these last few years asleep, not fully taking in all that was right there for me. So, I see it as a gift at these times, a very difficult gift, but still a gift".

Cris remarked how much the mood of the room changed as they let that message sink in. While still very sad, there was something else brought into the room as well. It gave them a way to move where they had been so stuck before.

So, what can we take from this view, this very personal precious moment in someone's life? For some, perhaps you, one helpful way to look at life's adverse, darkest times, is to look at them from a very different point of view; that instead of just pain and tragedy, there is something else in there that can add to who we are in important, even positive ways. This is the idea of a difficult gift.

Try to see whatever you are struggling with as a gift, not just a painful thing, as a very difficult thing that has been given you. It was not welcome; no one would want it, which is why it's a "difficult gift". Yet, because of it, we have been given something we would not have otherwise gotten. Perhaps it is an appreciation of how much others matter to us, how precious life is, how short our life may be, and how not to waste a moment. We would have preferred not to be made into this more patient, wiser, person with this perspective if the tragic event or trauma didn't occur, but that isn't a choice. So instead, try for a second to see if within the experience, something else has come that is in fact a gift. It may be a perception of life, an appreciation of others, or some quality in you that you never appreciated or even knew was there.

This story seems to fit so many things we've covered in this book; the ability to rethink our events, seeing the impact thoughts have on us. To not avoid, but to make room for the feelings and pain in our life. To live fully in the moment, in the present moment. To not struggle with what shows up, but to try to learn from it, as a human experience, which deserves a nuanced, complicated pattern. Who ever said it was easy or simple to be human? But, what else would we rather be?

"Being born a human being is a rare event in itself, and it is wise to use this opportunity as beneficially as possible."

- the Dali Lama

Why Not Me?

One cancer survivor I spoke with showed how within a minute of receiving her diagnosis, she had already answered the question "Why me?", with this new view "Why not me?". It had to be someone, and I'm the one. So, now what do I do? It gave her movement, and resolves to see herself as not stuck, or feeling bad, but moving toward how to deal with the illness, and how to live her life WITH the illness.

This flexibility in thinking, and moving to a new place for some people is so natural. Let's take a moment to see how it provided this woman with so much more than staying stuck with the unfairness of her being diagnosed with a frightening illness. She quickly moved to someone who is instead looking at what she can do right now, what her future direction needs to be, and is using all of her resources in service of the life she'd like to have, in whatever fashion is possible. She is not looking at a question or statement which is unanswerable, or mired in self blame (such as, "I knew that smoking would kill me," or "Why didn't I move away from those power lines?"). Thoughts that bring strong emotion and self blame, which often can not be proven, clearly are just self statements that can paralyze one with an inability to look towards ones values.

Advice to myself-

Leave the dishes.

Let the celery rot in the bottom drawer of the refrigerator

and an earthen scum harden on the kitchen floor.
Leave the black crumbs in the bottom of the toaster.
Throw the cracked bowl out and don't patch the cup.
Don't patch anything. Don't mend. Buy safety pins.
Don't even sew on a button.
Let the wind have its way, then the earth
that invades as dust and then the dead
foaming up in gray rolls underneath the couch.
Talk to them. Tell them they are welcome.
Don't keep all the pieces of the puzzles
or the doll's tiny shoes in pairs, don't worry
who uses whose toothbrush or if anything
matches at all.
Except one word to another. Or a thought.
Pursue the authentic—decide first
what is authentic,
then go after it with all of your heart.
Your heart, that place
you don't think of cleaning out.
That closet stuffed with savage mementos.
Don't sort the paper clips from screws from saved baby teeth
or worry if we're all eating cereal for dinner
again. Don't answer the telephone, ever,
or weep over anything at all that breaks.
Pink molds will grow within those sealed cartons
in the refrigerator. Accept new forms of life
and talk to the dead
who drift in through the screened windows, who collect
patiently on the tops of food jars and books.
Recycle the mail, don't read it, don't read anything
except what destroys
the insulation between yourself and your experience
or what pulls down or what strikes at or what shatters
this ruse you call necessity.

- Louise Erdich

Values – What is important to you?

Values are a topic that has been imbedded in all of this book. Why would anyone do the things that we are suggesting, that can cause such momentary suffering, with the goal of managing those feelings better? There has to a be a very personal reason. These are our values. We have things in life that matter to us, very personal reasons we are willing to go down this road. Reasons such as our loved ones and our relationships with them, our life's purpose, reasons such as helping others, our community, spiritual reasons, or just paths that allow us to acquire from life those experiences that hold meaning. This is why any of us are willing to walk the paths outlined in this book. Why we want to get out of the place where we are feeling so badly, and having our life so limited. But if those chains are taken off, what would you do? Where would you take yourself? Those are the paths that matter. Asking a question like "Why not me?" seems like one example where a very courageous woman is showing us a way to move in that direction. So, again, don't wait to feel better to do those things that matter; do them now and see if you'll feel better having done them. Either way, you're likely to at least say you did something today that held some value, no matter how small. It is a step in the direction that holds value.

Whether the following example is true or not, I leave to elephant trainers, but it was shared with me as true, and I share it with you so it may help you think about your habits and behaviors. The story involves how you train one of the world's most powerful animals, the elephant. What I was told, is that when they are young, elephants are bound by a long, heavy chain. The young elephant cannot escape it no matter how hard it tries. But, paradoxically, as the elephant gets older, the trainers use less strong restraints. Sometimes, just string, or even thread that's heavy enough to let the elephant know its there. The string will hold the elephant, even though in truth, it is strong enough to have broken even the thickest chains that bound it when it was young. Why? It appears that even elephants have minds that learn, and the learning from its youth leaves habits and associations that let the elephant know, "It can't possibly break free", so it doesn't even try. The real chain is in the mind, not what is placed around the leg!

"In one of the first teachings I ever heard, the teacher said, 'I don't know why you came here, but I want to tell you right now that the basis of this whole teaching is that you're never going to get it all together.' I felt a little like he had just slapped me in the face or thrown cold water over my head, but I've always remembered it. There isn't going to be some precious future time when all the loose ends will be tied up. Even though it was shocking to me, it rang true. One of the things that keeps us unhappy is this continual searching for pleasure or security, searching for a little more comfortable situation, either at the domestic level or at the spiritual level or at the level of mental peace."

- Pema Chodron

"It can't be helped."

I was riding home one day and I heard a story on the radio about the survivors of the 2011 tsunami in Japan and how the survivors were dealing with that horrific event. Besides enduring the tsunami, horrible enough all by itself, the water had destroyed the nuclear reactor, raising the risk and fear of possible nuclear disaster that just continued for weeks at a time. When asked how they were doing, one survivor described a Japanese word that roughly translated meant, "It can't be helped". He tried to explain how this was a word that helped them accept what had happened and not be stuck with the overwhelming events that at first examination would appear to be more than what anyone could just about bear.

Let's look at it how that phrase captures such a powerful feeling while allowing psychological movement, at least from the view of a psychologist hearing the story.

First, one needs to face the part of the event that lets you know that the situation is hopeless. Not in a despairing way, but in the inevitability of the event. One can't stop a tsunami, or the fallout of a nuclear reactor. No one can stop the radiation spreading into food, into water, or look for loved ones pulled out into the Pacific Ocean. There can be no help for you. There are no words, no actions that can undo those events. It can't be helped.

Related and imbedded in the phrase is the notion of fate. It is inevitable, and needs to be accepted. Interesting word, and interesting way to blend the two concepts together. It doesn't mean however, that the events and how you deal with them can't be transformed into something else, or that the path is determined. It is limited to the time it is occurring. It is very present focused. You and where you go are not hopeless, or inevitable; it's just those traumas that needed to be survived and then carried. It can't be helped, the scars will be there, but what happens next is not yet determined. You can have an effect.

Nietzsche Redux

The philosopher Frederick Nietzsche, who wrote, "That which does not kill me makes me stronger", I have recently discovered didn't truly find that quote applied to him. I was surprised that I learned that in his rather lonely life, he contracted syphilis and gradually became quite ill physically, until he was ultimately under the care of his sister. He was a frail, damaged man. The impact of his tragic illness, to most observers, left him weaker, both mentally and physically, not stronger.

In a recent article in Vanity Fair (January 2012) by Christopher Hitchens, an extremely sensitive and thoughtful counter argument is offered where one's illness, particularly a potentially terminal or chronic illness, can weaken one to the point where one is drained of their vitality and one is confronted with the losses that accumulate from the ravages of the illness.

My clinical experience bears out this reaction as well. While many of my patients' "put up a good fight", they get worn down by the energy, pain, losses, and suffering that can go into dealing with an illness or injury (both emotional as well as physical). So, what can anyone do to address this, and what information in this book might be of help?

- **First, I'll draw on the experience of embracing "small victories"**. There are in every day experiences, places where we can achieve some realization of those values or actions that matter to us. It might be an intimate moment with a friend or loved one that comes in a statement, or gesture that's given. Living in the "now" and realizing how life is not forever, gives us a way to savor all that is included. The idea of facing our own death is hard, and something most of us will struggle with. But it is also something we must all do. The way we deal with our fears, our thoughts, and feelings are all places where we can have a "small victory", which depending upon how you look at it is not small at all. I remember a patient who had been caught up in how he was unable to do the active physical things he so enjoyed before his illness advanced. Now he was forced to move very slowly, and couldn't climb stairs. Yet, once he put down the limits of what he had lost, and saw more clearly what was in front of him, he was able to claim "small victories" in sharing time with his children and wife who loved him. He was able to laugh, to cry, and to share some of life's most intimate moments that were still there.

- **Social support**. As we spoke of earlier, if one is lucky enough to have friends and family who care, they are indeed fortunate. It is an old truism that when one looks back on life, the most dear and important memories are those that include family, friends and those values that have mattered. Very few people wish they had spent more time at work, instead wishing they had done more of the things that matter. Use the lessons of social support.
- **Self-compassion**. Please be kind to yourself. Yes, we can all look at things we wish we had done differently. But in moments of need, try to treat yourself as you would someone you valued and loved.
- **Look at your thoughts and feelings**. Try to examine if the pain is needed. Some suffering is exactly where we need to be, but often the depth and frequency is more than one can or needs to bear. If your thoughts are possible to examine, change, or at least see for what they are, thoughts... perhaps you can impact how you able to deal with the present moment.

Perceptions and thoughts one more time

There is a story of a fisherman out on a foggy morning, and then he sees a boat slowly approaching him. At first he doesn't think much about it, but after awhile he sees the boat is in fact heading right towards him and his nets. He waits awhile, then yells out at the boat to be aware that he is there and to change course. But the boat keeps heading his way. Growing alarmed, he yells more loudly and more vigorously "Hey! Look out! You're going to hit my boat." But it continues, growing larger and larger, looming menacingly through the fog. Now he is angry and scared, if something doesn't happen this could be awful! But the boat continues towards him. There's nothing he can do, except yell, "What's wrong with you! Don't you know you're going to crash!" The fisherman prepares to move his boat out of the way, all the while yelling and wondering what kind of a jerk this other boat captain is! But, then as the other boat comes out of the fog, and passes just out of harms way, he sees... there is no captain. The boat is adrift, and had been proceeding unmanned. As the boat continues to drift out of sight, back into the fag, the fisherman laughs, and his feeling of anger leaves replaced by relief and a smile.

So, what happened here? As you'll recall it is not the events that bother us so much as how we perceive them. If the boat was captained by a bad skipper, one who could crash into a boat causing damage and even kill someone out at sea, then alarm is appropriate and the fisherman had every right to yell, and have his anger be present. But in this case there was no captain of the other boat. It was doing just what it had to do, drift. Once the fisherman realized this perception, the reasons for the anger left, the cause for danger was averted and relief and humor could arise. Of course it's totally human to react that way. But, it is possible to see how by being human, we react in ways that we can too soon leap to conclusions, not because of facts, but because of what we think are the facts. I hope you'll remember the fisherman, and how feelings shift and change, sometimes very quickly. It is a good lesson to see it is possible to accept things that are not controllable, and by that acceptance it is much easier to live with them.

We shall not cease from exploration
And the end of all our exploring
Will be to arrive where we started
And know the place for the first time.

- T.S. Eliot

CHAPTER FIFTEEN

Closing Remarks

More Honey Locust

Any day now
the branches
of the honey locust
will be filled
with white fountains;
in my hands
I will see
the holy seeds
and a sweetness
will rise up
from those petal-bundles
so heavy
I must close my eyes
to take it in,
to bear
such generosity.
I hope that you too
know the honey locust,
the fragrance
of those fountains;
and I hope that you too will pause
to admire the slender trunk,
the leaves, the holy seeds,
the ground they grow from
year after year
with striving and patience;
and I hope that you too
will say a word of thanks.

- Mary Oliver

In Pema Chodron's 2006 interview with Bill Moyers from his PBS show, she discusses waking up each day to say *"I wonder what will happen today,"* carrying that kind of curiosity through ones life.

She goes on to add,

"My teacher Trungpa Rinpoche encouraged us to lead our lives as an experiment, a suggestion that has been very important to me. When we approach life as an experiment, we're willing to try it this way and that way because, either way, we have nothing to lose.

This immense flexibility is something I have learned from watching Trungpa Rinpoche. His enthusiasm enabled him to accomplish an amazing amount in his life. When some things don't work out, Rinpoche's attitude was 'no big deal.' If it's time for something to flourish, it will; if it's not time, it won't.

The trick is not getting caught in hope and fear. We can put our whole heart into whatever we do; but if we freeze our attitude into for or against, we're setting ourselves up for stress. Instead, we could just go forward with curiosity, wondering where this experiment will lead."

- Pema Chodron from pbs.org/moyers/faithandreason/portraits_chodron.html.

As I write this final chapter, there are two things that have occurred that color my thoughts.

The first is that the first draft of this chapter was written the weekend of the 10-year remembrance of the 9/11 terrorist attacks on America. The country as a whole was asking, "How do we move through this tragic memory, these traumas?" In keeping with this book, "How do we transform this tragedy?" It is a very powerful experience as we see the survivors, and how they have carried this memory, and found ways to move forward. The saying provided earlier, "our scars show where we have been, not where we are going" is evident in the stories and memories of the past 10 years. No one should or could forget that day, or the days that followed. It is not only impossible, that is not the way our minds work, nor would it be appropriate as a way to deal with the courage and sacrifices of those who have dealt in the most personal way with those horrors and losses.

Yet transform we must. To stay as if time stood still emotionally would not be a path of growth. Much as in our bodies, change occurs all the time, with or without our awareness. I remember (accurately or not I leave to the biologists) that our bodies over the years will literally have changed nearly every cell in our body. We are literally not the person we were 10 years earlier. Yet, if you look at pictures of yourself when you were a child, and pictures of yourself now, you can still see "yourself". You are there, even with all the changes. That fact is an appropriate metaphor for how we change in ways other than our bodies.

"The ultimate authority must always rest with the individual's own reason and critical analysis."

- the Dalai Lama

I know I can recall, as can nearly everyone alive at the time, where I was on the day of 9/11/01 and the feelings it evoked in me as I went through the day, even though I was hundreds of miles away from the World Trade Center, and the Twin Towers in New York City, working in my office in Albany, NY. A gentleman I was seeing came into my office and asked, "If I'd heard that an airplane had crashed into one of the Twin Towers in New York City?" He then said he heard on the radio on his way over to the appointment, that the announcer had said it was possible it wasn't an accident, but that the country was under attack! Our session became secondary, and we left my office and went looking for any of the other doctors' offices that might have a television, so we could see what was going on. No one did. We eventually found a receptionist with a radio and asked her to turn it on to a news station and we all listened in disbelief to the events of the day unfold. I remember as I continued seeing patients that entire day, how it was impacting everyone; and I had my own internal urgency to call family, find out what they had heard, and to reassure myself that everything was ok, and we were safe. Except of course for that idea that no one could attack America, and that we were somehow protected by our national security and police, an idea which was shattered and gone, for at least this past decade.

Later, my colleague Dr. Ed Blanchard and I gave a number of workshops to mental health professionals on how to treat acute stress disorder (a version of PTSD that comes in the first 30 days after a trauma), PTSD, and other reactions to trauma in brief, empirically demonstrated models. While there was a team of mental health professionals who went to NYC and to Washington DC to help, the fallout of that day impacted lives for years afterward leading people to professionals to help deal with the memories that wouldn't leave, and the feelings that impacted their lives. We saw them in Albany too, as people who had lived in NYC left to come to Albany to "escape" and "feel safe" again. And in people who lived in Albany, but often commuted to NYC who had increased anxiety and fear join them the closer they got to the city. Again, what you've learned in this book was used to help each of those people deal more successfully with the impact of the trauma. One person who spent quite awhile with me, had just had her office relocated out of the twin towers the week before, and had moved into another skyscraper that gave her a clear view of her old office in the World Trade Center. She watched the whole horror unfold in front of her, including the people jumping from the burning offices. She knew a number of people who died that day, and couldn't get those images out of her mind, or the thoughts that it could very easily have been her in the offices if not for an act of fate.

The second event that influenced me, much less public, but an important one in professional circles, was an editorial published on August 3rd, 2011 by Dr. Charles Hoge, one of the most prominent experts on PTSD, in the Journal of the American Medical Association (JAMA). In that journal Dr. Hoge discussed our current understanding of how to treat PTSD and what it is that we really know. He concluded that when all is said and done we know this: in order for our treatment to be successful we need five core components, **1)** narration, **2)** cognitive restructuring, **3)** in vivo exposure, **4)** stress inoculation (e.g. relaxation skills), and **5)** psychoeducation. That as long as these components are applied, how they may be packaged is not important. They can be done verbally, in written form, by trained professionals or by lay counselors. I would even argue that the same techniques can be applied by traumatized individuals. I would argue that these components in fact are part of what makes the majority of people resilient to PTSD and helps the disorder improve if it does occur, and to resolve without the use of any mental health professionals. Because in one way or another, whether it is by our selves, pushing because we have to feed our families or not let our kids down; or because we have friends who cajole and push us back to health, the path to healing is walked frequently by those who have had to deal with life's traumas.

It is hoped that by the information shared in this book, that finding and walking on that path will be a little easier. Some people will need to work with mental health professionals. That's all right. As a psychologist who has had the opportunity to work with a variety of mental health professionals, I can say with great confidence, there is help out there to be found. Please seek it out if you believe you are in need.

I truly hope in some fashion this book touches and helps everyone who picks it up, whether someone dealing with a trauma, or someone who knows someone struggling with a personal tragedy. Learning about life's tragedies and how people can find a way through them is a good thing for everyone who has had their life touched by tragedy. I think that is nearly all of us in one way or another.

"It is said that if you want to know what you were doing in the past, look at your body now; if you want to know what will happen to you in the future, look at what your mind is doing now."

- the Dalai Lama

My own injuries and traumas in life have clearly left scars, and shaped who I am at this moment. I have learned how much we are all in this together. I certainly continue to have some lasting pain, and some days it is clearly worse than others. I have memories that I'd prefer not visit me, but I try to make room for them and to let them be a force that helps me be present with the experiences of my life. I hope the experiences have helped me become a better psychologist, teacher, husband, father, friend, and human being. I fully realize I have much more to learn and experience in whatever life holds for me. I hope I continue to have the excitement of wondering what each new day will bring.

All of the knowledge that is contained in this book is provided not so much by me, (I am just the vehicle), but instead came from the many thousands of people with who I have had the privilege to share this very personal, painful portion of their lives. I have endeavored in what ever way possible to be a guide in their courageous way back to a life that mattered to them, and one where they could suffer less the scars of their trauma. I know their experiences helped me with my own moments of need, and at this time I thank them for anything that was shared.

If you let negative emotions and thoughts arise inside you without any sense of restraint, without mindfulness of their negativity, then in a sense you are giving them free rein. However, if you develop mindfulness of their negativity, then when they occur, you will be able to stamp them out as soon as they arise. You will not give them the opportunity or the space to develop into full-blown negative emotional thoughts.

If a problem is fixable, if a situation is such that you can do something about it, then there is no need to worry. If it's not fixable, then there is no help in worrying. There is no benefit in worrying whatsoever.

Another result of spiritual development, most useful in day-to-day life, is that it gives a calmness and presence of mind. Our lives are in constant flux, bringing many difficulties. When faced with a calm and clear mind, problems can be successfully resolved.

- the Dalai Lama

"When it is dark enough, you can see the stars."

- Ralph Waldo Emerson

Share Your Story

We would like to hear your story of transformation. If you are willing please contact www.transformingtragedy.com, sign the needed release form and share your story with the Transforming Tragedy community.

References

As with this entire book, I have also approached the reference section somewhat non-traditionally. The material where I could provide a direct reference I did so by name within the book. There are also a number of references that over the years have become less clear where they came from, becoming incorporated into practice and a general understanding of this area. If I have not given credit where credit is thought do, I fully apologize now.

I also wanted the references to convey the broad reading and understanding of the area that went into the book. With that in mind I have added a number of books even if they were not direct sources, I know that their material somehow influenced my thinking and what was provided within the text.

In some places the material was not included in the text, but I believed so strongly in the work, that I wanted to provide it for you as well.

I hope you find these references and sources as useful and fulfilling as I did. Many of them led me down paths I never would have thought of until I stumbled across them in my wanderings.

I have tried to give interested readers some limited organization to the material. As my organizational scheme in this instance is also unconventional, it hopefully doesn't lead to extreme inefficiency in your efforts to get material. I invite you simply to try to receive these titles as they were given, as a source of information and wisdom that is now being passed from me to you.

Professional Books

American Psychiatric Association. Diagnostic and Statistical Manual of Mental Disorders (4th edition –text revision). Washington, DC: American Psychiatric Association, 2000.

Benson H. The Relaxation Response. New York, NY: Avon Books, 1975.

Bernstein, D.A. & Borkovec, T.D. Progressive Relaxation Training: A manual for the helping professions. Research Press. Champaign; IL, 1973.

Blanchard, E.B. & Hickling E.J. After the Crash: Psychological Assessment and Treatment of Survivors of Motor Vehicle Accidents (2nd edition). Washington, DC: The American Psychological Association, 2004.

Bryant, R.A. & Harvey, A.G. Acute Stress Disorder: A Handbook of Theory, Assessment, and Treatment. Washington, DC: American Psychological Association, 2000.

Calhoun, L.G. & Tedeschi, R.G. The Handbook of Posttraumatic Growth: Research and Practice. New York, NY: Lawrence Erlbaum Associates, 2006.

Foa, E.B. & Rothbaum, B.O. Treating the Trauma of Rape: Cognitive-Behavioral Therapy for PTSD. New York, NY: The Guilford Press, 1998.

Follette, V.M. & Pistorello, J. Finding life beyond trauma: Using acceptance and commitment therapy to heal from post-traumatic stress and trauma related problems. Oakland, CA: New Harbinger Publications, Inc., 2007

Frankl, V.E. Man's Search for Meaning. Boston, MA: Beacon Press., 2006.

Frankl, V.E. The Doctor and the Soul: From Psychotherapy to Logotherapy. New York, NY: Bantam Books, 1969.

Harris, R. ACT Made Simple: A Quick-start Guide to ACT basics and beyond. Oakland, CA: New Harbinger Publications, Inc., 2009

Hayes, S.C. & Smith, S. Get out of your mind & into your life. Oakland, CA: New Harbinger Publications, Inc., 2005.

Hickling, E.J. & Blanchard, E.B. The International Handbook of Road Traffic Accidents & Psychological Trauma: Current Understanding, Treatment and Law. Oxford, UK: Elsevier Science, Ltd., 1999.

Hickling, E.J. & Blanchard, E.B. Overcoming the Trauma of your Motor Vehicle Accident: A Cognitive-Behavioral Treatment Program (workbook). Oxford, UK: Oxford University Press, 2006.

Hickling, E.J. & Blanchard, E.B. Overcoming the Trauma of your Motor Vehicle Accident: A Cognitive-Behavioral Treatment Program (therapist guide). Oxford, UK: Oxford University Press, 2006.

Hoge, C.W. Once a Warrior Always a Warrior: Navigating the Transition from Combat to Home –including combat stress, PTSD, and mTBI. Globe Pequot Press, Guilford, CT, 2010.

Janoff-Bulman, R. Shattered Assumptions: Towards a New Psychology of Trauma. New York, NY: The Free Press, 1992.

Matsakis, A. I Can't Get Over It: a Handbook for Trauma Survivors. Oakland, CA: New Harbinger Publications, Inc., 1992.

Meichenbaum, D. Stress Inoculation Training. New York, NY: Pergamon Press, 1985.

Meichenbaum, D. A Clinical Handbook/Practical Therapist Manual for Assessing and Treating Adults with Posttraumatic Stress Disorder (PTSD). Waterloo, CAN: Institute Press., 1994.

Neff, K. Self Compassion: Stop Beating Yourself Up and Leave Insecurity Behind. William Morrow/Harper Collins: New York, 2011.

Olsen, P. Emotional Flooding: Volume I: New Directions in Psychotherapy. New York, NY: Human Sciences Press, 1976.

Pennebaker, J.W. Opening Up: The healing power of expressing emotion. New York: Guilford Press, 1997.

Resick, P.A. & Schnicke, M.K. Cognitive Processing Therapy for Rape Victims: A Treatment Manual. Newbury Park, CA: Sage Publications, 1993.

Rosen, G.M & Frueh, B.C. (Eds.) Clinician's Guide to Posttraumatic Stress Disorder, Hoboken, NJ: John Wiley and Sons, Inc., 2010.

Rothbaum, B.O. & Foa, E.B. Reclaiming your life after rape: Cognitive-behavioral therapy for posttraumatic stress disorder. Therapy Works: Graywind Publications Inc., The Psychological Corporation, 1999.

Walser, R.D. & Westrup, D. Acceptance & Commitment therapy of the Treatment of Post-Traumatic Stress Disorder & trauma Related Problems. Oakland, CA: New Harbinger Publications, Inc., 2007.

Wegner, D.M. White Bears and other Unwanted Thoughts: Suppression, Obsession, and the Psychology of Mental Control. New York, NY: The Guilford Press, 1994.

Yalom, I.D. Staring at the Sun: Overcoming the Terror of Death. San Francisco, CA: Jossey-Bass, 2009

Good Books

Armstrong, Lance. It's Not About the Bike: My Journey Back to Life. New York, NY: Berkley Books, 2001

Berra, Yogi. When you come to the fork in the road, take it. : Inspiration and wisdom from one of baseball's greatest heroes. New York, NY: Hyperion, 2001.

Chodron, Pema. The Places That Scare Us: a guide to fearlessness in difficult times. Boston, MA: Shambhala Publications Inc., 2001.

Chodron, Pema. The Wisdom of No Escape and the Path of Loving-Kindness. Boston, MA: Shambhala Publications Inc., 1991.

Hanh, Thich Nhat. Essential Writings. Maryknoll, NY: Orbis Books, 2001.

Hanh, Thich Nhat. Anger: Wisdom for Cooling the Flames. New York, NY, Riverhead Books, 2001.

Hanh, Thich Nhat. The miracle of mindfulness: An introduction to the practice of meditation. Boston, MA, Beacon Press, 1976.

Kabat-Zinn, Jon. Wherever you go there you are: Mindfulness meditation in everyday life. New York: NY, Hyperion, 1994.

Kushner, Harold S. When Bad Things Happen to Good People. New York, NY: Anchor Books, 1981.

Pirsig, Robert M. Zen and the Art of Motorcycle Maintenance: An Inquiry into Values. New York, NY: HarperTorch, 1999.

Tolle, Eckhart. A New Earth: Awakening to your life's purpose. New York, NY: A Plume Book, 2006.

Trungpa, Chogyam. Shambhala: The sacred path of the warrior. Boston, MA: Shambhala Publications Inc., 2003.

Voltaire. Candide. Toronto, CAN: 1959.

Watts, Alan. Become what you are. Boston, MA: Shambhala Publications Inc., 2003

Weil, Andrew. Spontaneous Healing: How to Discover and enhance your Body's natural Ability to Maintain and Heal Itself. New York, NY: The Ballantine Publishing Group, 1995.

Yalom, Irwin D. When Nietzsche Wept: A Novel of Obsession. New York, NY; Basic Books, 2003.

Zi, Nancy. The Art of Breathing: Thirty Simple Exercises for Improving Your Performance and Well-Being. Bantom Books, 1986.

Journal Articles

American Psychologist, January 2011, vol. 66 (1) Special Issue: Comprehensive Soldier Fitness.
Benish, S.G., Imel, Z.E., & Wampold, B.E. (2008). The relative efficacy of bona fide psycho-theapies for treating post-traumatic stress disorder: a meta-analysis of direct comparisons. *Clinical Psychology Review, 28*, 746-758.

Bonanno, G.A. (2008). Loss, trauma, and human resilience: Have we underestimated the human capacity to thrive after extremely aversive events? *Psychological Trauma: Theory, Research, Practice and Policy, Vol. S (1),* 101-113.

Blanchard, E.B., Hickling, E.J., Devineni, T., Veazey, C.H., Galovski, T.E., Mundy, E., Malta, L.S. & Buckley, T.C. (2003). A controlled evaluation of cognitive behavioral therapy for post traumatic stress in motor vehicle accident survivors. *Behavior Research and Therapy, 41*, 79-96

Ehlers, A. & Clark, D.M. (2000). A cognitive model of post-traumatic stress disorder. *Behaviour Research and Therapy, 38*, 319-345.

Friedman, M.J., Resick, P.A., Bryant, R.A., Strain, J., Horowitz, M. & Spiegel, D. (2011), Classification of trauma and stressor related disorders in dsm-5, depression and anxiety, 28, 737-749.

Hoge, C.W. (2011). Interventions for war-related posttraumatic stress disorder: Meeting veterans where they are. *Journal of the American Medical Association, 306*, 549-551.

Keane, T.M., Zimering, R.T., & Caddell, J.M. (1985). A behavioral formulation of post-traumatic stress disorder. *Behavior Therapist, 8*, 9-12.

Lang, P.J. (1977). Imagery in therapy: An information processing analysis of fear. *Behavior Therapy, 8*, 862-886.
Lang, P.J. (1979). A bio-informational theory of emotional imagery. *Psychophysiology, 16,* 495-512.

Mowrer, O.H. (1947). On the dual nature of learning: The reinterpretation of "conditioning" and "problem solving." *Harvard Educational Review, 17*, 102-148.

Neff, K.D. (2003). Development and validation of a scale to measure self-compassion. *Self and Identity, 2,* 223-250.

Neff, K.D. (2003). Self-compassion: An alternative conceptualization of a healthy attitude toward oneself. *Self and Identity*, *2*, 85-102.

Resick, P.A., Galovski, T.E., O'Brien-Uhlmansiek, M, Scher, C.D., Clum, G., Young-Xu, Y. (2008). A randomized clinical trial to dismantle components of cognitive processing therapy for posttraumatic stress disorder in female victims of interpersonal violence. *Journal of Consulting and Clinical Psychology, 76*, 243-258.

Rutter, M. (1987). Psychosocial resilience and protective mechanisms. *American Journal of Orthopsychiatry, 57*, 316-331.

Schnurr, P.P., Lunney, C.A., & Sengupta, A. (2004). Risk factors for the development versus maintenance of posttraumatic stress disorder. *Journal of Traumatic Stress, 17,* 85-95.

Tedeschi, R.G. & Calhoun, L.G. (2004). Posttraumatic growth: Conceptual foundations and empirical evidence. *Psychological Inquiry, 15*, 1-18.

Tedeschi, R.G. & Calhoun, L.G. (1996). The posttraumatic growth inventory: measuring the positive legacy of trauma. *Journal of Traumatic Stress, 9,* 455-469.

Thompson, B.L. & Waltz, J. (2008). Self-compassion and PTSD symptom severity. *Journal of Traumatic Stress, 21*, 556-558.

Tolin, D.F. & Foa, E.B. (2006). Sex differences in trauma and posttraumatic stress disorder: a quantitative review of 25 years of research. *Psychological Bulletin, 132*, 959-992.

Tolin, D.F. & Breslau, N. (2007). Sex differences in risk of PTSD. *NCPTSD PTSD Research Quarterly, 18 (2),* 1-8.

Vrana, S.R. & Lauterbach, D. (1994). Prevalence of traumatic events and post-traumatic psychological symptoms in a non-clinical sample of college students. *Journal of Traumatic Stress, 7*, 289-302.

Online Resources

http://www.apa.org/helpcenter/resilience-war.pdf

http://www.apa.org/helpcenter/road-resilience.aspx

www.melissainstitute.org (for downloadable texts from Donald Meichenbaum, including: Understanding Resilience in Children and Adults: Implications for Prevention and Interventions

www.ncptsd.gov

www.selfcompassion.org

www.contextualpsychology.org

Images

Images were obtained from Google Images using a commercially permissible license for reuse in the advanced search engine, and from Zuleikha Hester, who's creativity and generosity is greatly appreciated.

Images of the phoenix, including the cover image and logos were created by the author, and professionally augmented by Patrick Branigan. The image of the elephant was also created by the author for use in this text. All images contained within this work are protected by both copyright and trademark laws where applicable.

Edward J. Hickling, PsyD is an internationally known psychologist, author and lecturer. He has specialized in the area of post trauma disorders and psychological treatments. He received his Doctor of Psychology degree from the University of Denver in clinical psychology. He was Director of Training and consultation liaison psychologist at the Veterans Administration Medical Center in Albany, New York until he left to enter full time private practice. He has held academic positions at the Sage Colleges in Troy, NY, the University at Albany, State University of New York, Albany Medical College, and most recently at the University of South Florida.

Dr. Hickling is a master therapist, having practiced for over 30 years. He has given workshops at leading national and international conferences, as well as teaching students, interns, fellows and other professionals in the varied positions he has held. Most of his career was spent in Albany, NY where he maintained a thriving practice, taught at local universities, and conducted research with his good friend, colleague, and distinguished professor emeritus in psychology at the University at Albany, Dr. Edward Blanchard. He held a position as a research psychologist at the James A. Haley Veterans Hospital, Tampa, Florida, until his recent move to join the Center for Sexual Trauma Services at the Bay Pines, VA. He has maintained a consultation and private practice in both New York and Florida. He continues to be active in cutting edge research, teaching and the provision of psychological services, including telemental health.

Made in the USA
Middletown, DE
30 December 2014